Here's to the Land

*A Celebration
of
60 Years
by the
N.C. Poetry Society*

Edited by
Judith Holmes Settle

Editor

Judith Holmes Settle

Published by
The North Carolina Poetry Society

For information address:
The Pilot, Sam Ragan, Editor
P.O. Box 58
Southern Pines, NC 28388

ISBN 0-9633529-0-3 cloth
ISBN 0-9633529-1-1 paper
Library of Congress Catalog Card Number: 92-61147

Cover design: Elizabeth Hoyt

Typeset by: Eric Smith and Beverly Van Dyke
Makeup by: Frank Harris

Members who guided the formative planning of this
anthology are: Marie Gilbert, Judith Settle, Marsha Warren,
Robert Collins, Ray Dotson, Sam Ragan and Shelby
Stephenson.

Printed in the United States of America

Foreword

By Sam Ragan

A strong sense of place is a defining quality in the best of Southern, and North Carolina, prose and poetry. Add to this the emphasis on people and a heightened awareness of time by a great many poets and we have a natural division of the poetry contained in this volume, published to celebrate the 60th anniversary of the North Carolina Poetry Society.

The Society was formed in 1932, and it is not coincidental that what was to become the official State Toast was brought to light in the Legislature about the same time. The toast, officially adopted 25 years later, was written by two homesick Tar Heels—Leonora Martin and Mary Burke Kerr—then living in Richmond, Virginia, for a dinner attended by other displaced North Carolinians.

We have borrowed from the first of a four-stanza poem for our title and division allusions in this collection. Those lines are:

> Here's to the land of the long leaf pine,
> The summer land where the sun doth shine,
> Where the weak grow strong and the strong grow
great,
> Here's to "Down Home," the Old North State!

It seems a fitting salute to our state, our poetry society and its history, and to the 193 poets and the poems they personally chose for this Anniversary Celebration Collection.

Things were stirring then and now.

Preface

By Marie Gilbert

President

An anthology was among the first thoughts in planning the celebration of our sixtieth year. Each member of the North Carolina Poetry Society has been invited to submit one best poem in January of 1992.

Before the Anthology Committee finishes the process of producing this volume, the North Carolina Poetry Society will be into a new fiscal year and will have installed new officers - an indication of a healthy entity that absorbs energy from many, and from continuity, gathers strength far beyond that of any individual.

Born in the depth of the Great Depression, survivor of four wars, the poetry society has stood as a resource for poets and readers of poetry in difficult times as well as joyous times. We review our past in appreciation, and to set the line straight and true into the future. We celebrate the richness of the heritage upon which we build.

This book is offered as a chronicle of our art in our time. May it say to the future what we were and what we are, and become a cherished volume.

Here's to the Land

Contents

TIME

PEOPLE

Place

Here's to "Down Home"....

Mary C. Snotherly

Starlings: The Dark and Light Of It

November skies blacken
with sudden spills of starlings.
Swarms of them flock ceaselessly
out of the distance,
bank in against the light
to swell the sycamore,
to fill the emptied spaces
among last leaves.
And the tree sings.

They filter through fence rails,
speckle the field,
forage for seed.
Silver, lilac, green
feathers shimmer like mica.
Hundreds of eyes
glint gold.

Drawn to farther fields,
they lift in swirls
like metal dust to magnets.
Their multiple rust voices
rise in one enormous voice
hoarse as the grating of chains.
Hunger drums louder
than all their calls.

And after,
a spray of milkweed down
sifts weightlessly
and slow.
Spurs of white light
bless the earth again
mute as early snow.

Elizabeth Roberts

Images

Kudzu invades a red clay ditch
decorates a split rail fence
challenges a billboard.
The creeping vine
blankets meadows, shrouds bushes
and sprints up guy wires
to create a kingdom of Dr. Seuss characters.

Gladys Owings Hughes

Wings

Among angel and lamb monuments we read
century-old epitaphs   come up
with a few of our own, laughing so hard
we must rest against granite
and the stone-cold jolts us back
to the bony truth of this place.
Quick! Look for some signs of life!
(Play dead, Death)

    Mosses and lichens flourishing,
    clumps of white violets, pale
    pink forget-me-nots under
    the blue-berried cedars, and then
the nest, shallow as a saucer,
at the foot of a towering angel.

The kildeer flutters past us, one wing
trailing in sand to fake injury,
to lure us from the life
in her four cone-shaped eggs.
We move away   wish we could assume
her lightness as she rises high,
riding the silk of April air
giving her plaintive cry
"Kill-dee! Kill-dee! Dee - Dee - Dee!"
and we are joined in a splendid daring
to cherish life
here in the midst of death.

Debra Kaufman

Blinders

The man who invented blinders
knew the allure
of the pacers' slick flanks,
the swish and flash
of the drivers' bright satins,
knew to win you had to feel
only your own blood racing,
your own measured breath,
muscles straining against the reins.
What do you suppose that man said
to make his horse tremble
before the dash?
I almost asked you this morning
in that still moment between
folding the newspaper
and grabbing your coffee cup
to rush to the car,
where you'll only end up
skittish in the lineup
on the freeway.

Shirley Moody

Nourishment

I know mimosa leaves will close
if I touch them with my hands,
and I admit that once I drowned a pet turtle
thinking to clean it in a basin of water too warm --
a palm tree painted on its shell.

I know that I grew a little tree in
the backyard with a seed spit from
an orange Mother made me eat for breakfast
one May morning before she fell in bed
sedated after having nursed a patient
the night before. With tinctured breath
she proclaimed the tree would never grow.

But I also know that late that summer,
after potting the miracle sapling to bring inside
before frost, I held a magnifier against a leaf
thinking to give an extra boost of sunshine.
Then suddenly I watched as it smoked
and turned like anemic gardenias
Mother warned I'd bruise if I breathed
too near their petals.

And after our mother cat was run over,
I know that Mother and I cut an opening
too large in the bottle's nipple
drowning a kitten. And now I accept
that Mother and I, without either of us
knowing it, were complicitous in nature.

Pepper Worthington

I Owe Them

I owe them.
I could not be here in a room of my own
Were it not for them.

Locked in the frozen village of Massachusetts,
Anne Bradstreet stood tall, unflinching,
Writing her poetry in the face of poverty and loneliness.
Two centuries later Emily Dickinson created word-worlds,
Wrapped them in pink ribbons and waited for fame.
Another century crashed by
With a new pioneer, an echo of the past:
Edna St. Vincent Millay caught the Pulitzer Prize
Earned by women centuries before her
But not given.
I owe them.

America contains buckets of women with pioneer passion:
Carry Nation stomped her temperance through men
While Lucy Stone and Susan B. Anthony tore their hair
To get the vote for the second sex.
Harriet Sewall and Elizabeth Cady Stanton were fierce
In their fight for votes and justice for blacks.
Pioneer fire flooded them, made them bold,
Brave as the ideas they believed in.
I owe them.

They have made it easier for me,
Made it possible,
Made what once was a submerged ache
Now a chartered achievement.
I could not be here in a room of my own
Were it not for them.
I owe them.

Nina A. Wicker

This Line Forms to the Left

The next time you get caught in a line
perk up an ear, you might enjoy what you hear.
It happened to me:
The seafood was smelling good and hot all the way
to the parking lot when a long-haired intellect
chose to interject,

"This establishment would do a Wall Street
business if it wasn't daily capacitated."
And then there was the sure-footed, here-I-come-world
girl who pounded anxiously on the attendant's desk.

"Has the next plane left yet?"
In the theater line the other night two old lovebirds
cooed and patted as if they were out of sight when
suddenly he quipped for all to hear,

"So, I have insomnia, but it ain't nothing to
lose sleep over, dear."
During the holidays I stopped in a woodcarving shop
and a busy little clerk offered this friendly crack,

"If you see anything that isn't there, we probably
have more in the back."

Josephine M. Upchurch

The Unchanging Things

Things will never change in this valley.
There will be fog in the morning
The silent river, forgotten footprints.
Rains will brush vigorous grasses
and soapstone rocks in sunlight
bear carvings older than Rome.

Loneliness heavy as smoke
will fall like a curtain at sundown.
A screech owl will shatter the silence
With his awesome nightsong.

Nothing will ever be different here
only the change of the seasons --
solemn removal of golden September
by wilting autumnal rain
and frigid anger of winter
allayed by the greening willow tree.

Time will be chased away by the seasons
while faded eyes gaze at a sunset
after stormclouds in a startling July.
Summer will flee like a galaxy -- and
September will come again, and again,
and again.

Susan Slattery

Aunt Pat

We watched her ashes swirl in the current to the Tappan zee
until the lawyer waved us back to the white stucco house
where the day lady was scraping gray clay off Aunt Pat's wheel.
Pastel slivers and chalk remnants nestled in newspapers
with her gouge and chisels in a bureau's narrow drawers.

Poor nephew had planned to retire to this house, some clucked.
His drudge daughter-in-law thrust prayer cards in our faces.
In another room the elders divided the bronze and Kashmiri.
After we shook the books out, we stood a silent moment
in front of piles. Under the attic's trap door we reached up
for tapestries not unfolded since the missions to India.

At day's end I kissed the air beside my mother's cheek
and drove East until I heard the high whine of tires on metal.
Fighting vertigo, I snuck a fast glance at the water below
before fixing my sights on signs to Stamford and on beyond.

Eve Carol Shy

Professor Emeritus

The Great Blue Heron,
a child's S scrawled
across slate-sky,
visited our pond
each winter.

As he landed, his wings flapped
in a flurry -- chalkboard eraser
clapping together.
Hunched, he stood among the rushes,
his head retracted, a don

watching the school at his feet,
the only thing moving,
his ruffled boa
more frayed each year.

This winter,
the pond reflects
only sky
and rushes.

Dot Seibert

For Tim

Dreams are fragile things.

Morning fogs dashed upon the rocks
Returning, sadder, to the sea;

The gentle loon's soft evening call
Silent before man's mad midnights;

The boy child with the poet's eyes
Choosing his suicide weapon.

Dreams, like fog and loons and poets,
Should have little white tags that say

Do not touch.

Peter A. Saitta

Small Southern Towns
For Dorothy Mae

Courthouse shadows granted respite
from August's tumid heat; laden
with the smells of cured tobacco.
He would leave me where the old negro
ladies gathered, while he sought out
the barbershop across the street;
no place for little boys there, what
with cuspidores, and the strident talk
of politics and such.

She would care for me, that aging black
madonna, as she sold her gladiolus from
coffee cans beneath the statue's feet;
a monument to some long forgotten Rebel;
and, when the sun bore down, she would ask
"Ain't you parched chile?" and I would
answer "Yes ma'am," jumping down from
the courthouse steps.

Matchstick arms would boost me up
to work the marble fountain.
Then bending low, she would purse her
wrinkled lips and draw her own long drink.
I would always ask if I might taste
the water from her fountain.
She would always answer,
"Someday, chile...someday."

Annella Moore Rockson

The Source

Wind in their sails brought them here,
Far from the homeland they knew,
And now only the wind remains.

The Wright brothers sought it...
They channeled Kill Devil wind
To send men on further voyages,
Conquering air as the English did the waves.

Now children catch the wind in their kites.
They tumble down wind-swept hills of sand
That bury a long-lost farm.

The sand shifts;
But still remains the wind,
The spirit behind the land
Before the land itself.

Royce Ray

Preservation Hall

Soul soaring sounds
tingle my heart,
itch my feet.
Meld gold of black,
ebony of white,
sweet of low,
high of high
Bourboun (100-proof) Street.
Trumpet wide the pearly gates,
drum the bottom out of hell.
Hand it out,
take it back,
hand it out again.
Turn me inside out;
fold me skin to skin;
soft beat my heart
inside again.

Claire Atkins Pittman

Look Carefully

However you come to this,
you will not be prepared,
not for the dark eyes
of the Grand Duchesses
Anastasia and Marie
set in faces pale
as the milk-white enamel
encasing them,
not for the first Communion dress,
the single strand of pearls,
not for the Tsar and Tsarina,
pain smoothed from their brows
by the click of a camera,
their portraits frozen in diamonds
beneath a garland of gold.

Hold a moment, look carefully
at the small boy in the sailor suit,
serene for the eyes of forever;
this is the tsarevich Alexis,
born with the bruised blood of Kings,
caught in the tragic skein
of a history shattered in bullets
piercing the heart of the world.

Locked behind windows of glass,
fragile as flowers in ice,
the Romanovs stare from
their jewelled settings
into the staring eyes of strangers.

Here there is peace,
while outside worlds shift,
collide along the fault of history,
opened at Ekaterinburg.

Lola Lee Pack

The Survivor

After a wrong right turn took
My need ten lost road-map-miles south
I got directions from a local
Turning over hills south of Seattle
In nineteen hundred and forty-six -
A middleaged taker of auctioned tractors
Roto tillers and hybrid mules.
A hillside staker of winesap cider whips
And vinefera canes for wines.
An esthetic tamer of flame-red
Black-throated orientals
Caged on mounds inside
A circle of summer stocks
Bunched together in plastic cuffs
For rooms off hospital corridors.
A weeder of apologies.
An oil tanker widow
From the second world rehearsal
Of the battle at Armageddon.

Mary Elizabeth Nordstrom

Unlaundered Cache

Discovered in sand:
A deposit of dollars
With sculpted design.

Gathered-up treasure:
Salty seashells in pockets
As gifts for our friends.

Sand dollars on doorstep
Drying in bright summer sun:
The gift of the sea!

Sam McKay

Weymouth is Real

From the gray guards at the gate,
those sisyphean sentries,
to the shimmering fish in the pool;
from the historic conifers, scraping the sky,
to the fruitless cherries parading by the garden,
weeping as they go, tresses trembling mournfully,
to the tall white columns that blindly march
in line with the weeping cherries,
empathizing with their gravity;
from the fields of green
and the flowers that border the walkways,
to the graceful Boyd House arches
whose bases grasp the earth and, as it were,
lift it to heaven
where their crowns always point.

From the great room where many friends meet
joyfully promoting the arts,
surrounded by archways and antiques
that speak of periods and persons past,
to rambling stairways and hallways that lead
 to bedrooms, square rooms, long rooms
and even little surprise rooms,
just like flowers you didn't know were there
until they bloom.
And if, in this hallowed house,
conscious of the renowned writers
who lingered here a while,
you can be still, relax, and listen,
perhaps you will hear voices strange,
yet familiar because of what they say.

Soon your passing the gray guards at the gate
will be like the rushing of one born here.

Kay McClanahan

Peacocks in Tennessee

Grandmother kept peacocks.
Peafowl, she called them.
They stayed in the henyard
Between the toolshed and the barn,
Looking lost and abandoned,
Among the milkweed and woeful cedar.

A long time ago
The land was harsh,
And people struggled to live.
But still, she kept her birds
Knowing they were delicate
And terribly unwise. Good only
For their lovely plumes.

Grandmother, wearing her sunbonnet,
As was the fashion in her day,
Would call to them
Like one speaking to fine ladies.

Elinore F. McCaskill

The Monster on Highway 15-501

A monster rages down Highway 15-501,
Long, yellow, greedy snout
Searching the maw of earth
For roots, grasping and pulling
Earth's vitals from her bowels, pale, shredded.

Ancient Grendel, hideous, bilious yellow,
Man-driven, daily eight-hour humanoid.
With jerking gears, screeching tracks
Leaves void all in its path,
Crushed and twisted, doomed to die.

Then comes concrete mixer with gravel and lime,
Spewing forth mouthfuls of dough-colored slush,
Disgorging itself upon the naked, scraped earth.
Liquid density, hardening, covering,
Molded into a dull, smooth surface.

The serene silence of village and pine grove,
The muffled noise of diesels on the Circle.
The jackhammer staccato of red-cockaded woodpecker,
The tiny woodland flower and graceful honeysuckle vine
Shall fall before concrete's expanse and traffic's roar.

One day when Earth is a weaving of sterile, concrete ribbon,
And the monster with the snake-like snout
Stands idle with little to devour,
For root and tree and flower are no more.
We'll tell our children how it was back then
When there was a stand of trees in the Circle
And Black-eyed Susans along the shoulders of 15-501.
When our hearts would dance with the lilting birdsongs,
And there was a safe crossing from east to west
And from north to south on Highway 15-501.

Dorothy McCartney

New Peas in a Pod

What do <u>they</u> know of earth's sweet soil,
boiling about on those hard dead-white cement steps
in their tardy past-bedtime tenement play,
their pep
surely grown out of no earthy knowledge
of gooseberries swelling on a bush in the sun,
the aroma of fresh black-raspberry pie
when done, or even (my god!)
the look of ripe new peas in a pod...
except for that clever vegetable-pillow toy
  with its row of fat green legumes which lay
  in a matching green felt pod
that a richer Aunt Royetta gave away
to Willow McCoy on her last, her sixth, birthday?

Joy Murphy

On a Train From Copenhagen
Across Northern Germany, October, 1990

Layered gray clouds
Banded by blue,
Form a cieling above this flat land
Near the sea.
Red roofed houses scatter over green pastures,
Near brown plowed fields, and green rows of sugar beets.
Canals, water brimmed to the top,
Cut straight paths in the Northern German landscape.
Horses and cows linger in the dusk.
Houses with attached barns
Await the approach from the East.

Dolly Murphy

Becoming

Becoming
As the wish upon
A stillness within —
Dancing in the meadow
Kissing this and that
Drifting in the breeze
Finding a bubbling brook
Sipping amid the rock
Flittering with the spray.

Birthing from cocoon
The way of metamorphosis
Same and different
The worm and butterfly.

Domus

Bonnie Michael

Grandma's House

Her spirit is ploughed under
with the ashes of her home;
their energies are joined again.

She never knew the house was gone,
kept it inviolate in her mind,
did not see the consuming fire.

But the order was wrong; the house
should have died after she did,
not with her thoughts still in it.

The new grass is too green,
its lush growth the only sign
that anything else ever lived here.

I want to mark this passage for her
with Gabriel's trumpet, but maybe
the wind in the grass is enough.

Nannette Swift Melcher

Moving Would Be Easier if I Were a Turtle

Some people
live in the same town
all their lives
their roots go down to China
their junk goes up to the attic
to stay
forever.

"Move?" some people cried
"to a place you've never lived
where you don't know a soul?"
they pulled in their fences
and pulled down their shades
to keep out
change.

I packed
twenty-two boxes of books
pots and pans
cushioned china and glass in paper
crammed clothes into bureau drawers
sorted, saved
tossed out.

Now I live
where roses reach up to the pines
surrounded by people
who don't know a soul
we open our doors
reach out our hands
new roots
grow.

Richard de los Mar

Harbor

The day my grandfather died,
I smoked my first cigarette
squatting on hay
musty as a root cellar.
Outside, hogs
panted in their pens,
and far off the moonlight
glistened on miles of old fence.

At the hospital that night,
his oxygen tent
billowed like a sail, hoses
like ropes moored him to his bed.
I waited, listening
to the plastic bellows
and counted, remembering
his breath like smoke,
cold over the corn stalks.

Brenda C. Lawlor

Mercer's Lily Fields

Day lilies everywhere
brilliant yellows, reds, scarlets
profuse green foliage
birds and butterflies
dipping in the air

People milling through
oohing,
ahhing
carrying a piece of the garden
from the peace of the garden
hoping
it will take root

Catherine W. Lane

Bas-Relief: Aesculapius, God of Medicine

Mortar, stone, Greek-Roman Gods
   your scroll charts you.
Aphrodite tantalizes you
   to prancing spirits of the chase.
You are grand. Appollorized.

But you, O horrified Aesculapius,
   how your gods betrayed you.
Framed twixt spitting snakes, entwining staffs,
   symbols of your art,
The torture in your imprisoned eyes
   streams down in sightless tears.
I feel them drop....

Thunderbolts
   crackling through these majestic hills.
Zeus banished you. The Romans claimed you.
   Suffering, disease, injustice bowed you.
A cripple
   Man knew you not.

Born Greek Asclepius, physician,
   an infantile fantasy-bound id
      made you god.
   Jealousy doomed you to strange sullied sod
      and from this agonized soil, I know you.
   My soul reaches out to enfold your hurt
      but I hear only your breathless cry

Resounding through these majestic hills:
   The chafing winds burnt away my wings
   Ashes to ashes go gods and kings
   Let me live life WOMAN with MAN
   And when I die
        FREED As dust to dust
        GO I....

Hal Kome

Monument Valley

I found too many secrets in your rock,
they have colored me the color of blood,
a cold color and small.
I need one of your ewes around me
to make me warm, I need to curl up
inside her, my sheep mother,
to listen to her maa and understand her.
Why is your sky so heavy, so thick?
I feel that I could not put my hand
into it, it makes me afraid for the birds
who fly through it.
You are always too young, you are always
too old, because you have always been here,
because you were made yesterday.
There is too much edge to you,
the grass is afraid of you.
                    Look, when I
drop you my hand is dry, your color
does not wet me. I ask myself,
where are your eyes?
I am a twin with that lizard
who runs across you on tiptoe;
we will make our own destinations,
we will not always see you.

Mae B. Knight

My Home on Whiskey Creek

It's right on the water, twice a day.
Right on a mud hole, twice a day.
   Tides are funny, aren't they?

When the tide goes out, so does my view.
When the tide comes back, my view does too.
I don't cry when the tide goes out;
It'll come back in with a great big shout!

My home's great -- just right for me.
It's right on the water, twice a day.
   Tides are funny, don't you agree?

My life's like that; good and bad.
Sometimes great, sometimes sad.
Sometimes up, sometimes down.
   So why get stuck with a great big frown?

Yes, my life's just right for me.
So, I don't cry when the tide goes out;
It'll come back in with a great big shout!

Right on the water, twice a day.
Right on a mud hole, twice a day.
   Tides are funny, aren't they?

Earl Carlton Huband

Lost

Do not condemn this granite.
Become one with the stone
and weep as water trickles
down the cracks in its face.

Look for your reflection
in the pool of moving water
at the bottom of the stone.

Elizabeth S. Hoyt

Tethered

I used to bear left at Martin's Mill
go on about a mile to the light
   (now there are three)
through the arch of royal oaks
   (now Main Street is broader but treeless)

I'd turn left at the light
go to the white gabled house
midway the third block
   (now it's colonial blue)

deceiving from the street
a narrow high-ceilinged structure
but spacious enough to comfortably rear
half a dozen

and all six remained
tethered to it
sixty years more or less
tangled in each others' days

I'd follow aromas down the long hall
to the perpetual coffee pot
perhaps fresh angel food cake
partake, stay a while

my tether now is longer
I move in a wider circle
on a heavy chain

now when I come to Martin's Mill
I bear right

David Hood

Silence in the Sanctuary

There's a presence in the old churches
where the wooden pews are polished
by the flow of a thousand Sundays.

Stand alone in the sanctuary
with a vibrating silence
like the sudden hush
the half-second after
the organ stops its bellow.
Close your eyes. Listen.
You can almost hear
horses snort outside
while serious bearded men
share rumors and fears
of the war in Virginia.

The sense of being caught
in the compelling current
of something long in time
and powerful in memory
like floating down a river
going somewhere....

Open your eyes to silence
and dust motes dance
on a shaft of colored light.

Wrap the silence close
like a coat against the cold.
Turn and go outside.
Crows caw lonely in the cornfields,
and a car roars by on the road.

Muriel Hoff

No Dreaming Allowed

She crossed 42nd St. and Times Square
reminiscing about V-J Day,
servicemen laughing, crying, throwing
their arms around complete strangers,
and Tom bending her into a pretzel,
kissing the very breath out of her.

The hit-and-run driver left her
on the icy street. She saw the thief
lifting her wallet, the witnesses
melting away like the snow matting
her bloody hair, and the bag lady
pausing to nod in sympathy.

The construction workers, steel angels,
climbed down their ladders to shield
her from the oncoming traffic.
The ambulance skidded to a halt,
and she thought that on such a cold day
she should be home making chicken soup.

Robert R. Hentz

Touring East Tennessee, 1944-45

First saw the area with my thumb,
a college boy from a city
set in midwestern plains.
Stationed in the mystery city
born full-fledged from Einstein's head,
we roamed far afield on off days
enchanted by the mountain people,
the rural and rugged terrain.
Saw the Norris and Loudon TVA dams,
Gatlinburg when it was real,
and explored the glories of the Smokies.
Got as far as Lynchburg
one cold, gray, snowy day
and went south to Chattanooga
for a look at Lookout Mountain.
Had the Dayton courthouse pointed out,
where Darwin was denied,
by our gaunt old grizzled driver
hauling a load of pigs to market.
A future wife shared some such rides
hitched around the countryside,
back of a pickup with a farm-couple's kids,
bouncing on a flatbed, snug in a trucker's cab,
or in the comfort of an occasional car.
A good way to see the country,
not always knowing or caring
where you were going.
Things were different then,
the people friendly, sharing.
Country wasn't full of madmen.
"Give a soldier a ride," the posters said.
Almost everyone did.

Elinor O. Gray

Round Trip

It can't be helped, of course. They scoot across
one's path...no time for slamming on the brake
when THUD...another tabby's killed...   <u>small</u> loss!
What difference does one less kitten make?
Annoying how that frantic little pup
keeps skittering around among the cars;
some mongrel mixture not worth picking up....
Tonight, returning home beneath the stars
I see a small black form, its wagless tail
now crushed; and farther on a ginger cat
lies dead. At this late hour my wits are stale,
my thoughts on cozy hearth and fireside chat....
But even though I hear no piper's tune,
a myriad furry shapes <u>scoot</u> toward the moon.

Eugene V. Grace

The Old Man and the Tree

The old man wanted his lawns trim,
large lawns which each day beckoned him.
He remained true, all summer through,
and brought them neatly into fall.
On some days he mowed near an oak,
also old, hollow and lifeless,
whose gnarled and knuckled arms dripped
loose, grey bark upon the dead roots,
retained some like tattered clothing,
like that which fitted the old man.
One wondered when, not if, the fall.
The man once said it mattered not
in which slant of light he would cease,
and in each hour of the day
the sun shadowed limbs on the lawn;
by equinox he had seen each,
every silhouette the tree would make,
the reach and lean of each figure
that seemed more and more like his own.
On the last cutting of the year
he came close until he was near
the tree which had waited for him.

Evalyn Pierpoint Gill

Focus Between Poles

Arachnid hung in space,
miniscule crab reaching for limits of air,
caught
like an ancient coin
thrown on the winds,
I study your rorschach pattern
still but alive
and step aside to view obliquely
the sparkling wheel
balanced between pivot boxwoods
holding you fast
A breeze passes through the delicate maze,
your legs retract to a mottled disc.
I gather strength
from your tough survival
through aeons,
sturdy against our frail grasp
of this fragile planet.

Anna-Carolyn Stirewalt Gilbo

Japan 1991

I would tell you
how it feels
to sing Silent Night
with eight small Japanese children
who struggle with the strange sounds
I taught them,
to kneel on fragrant tatami mats
and discuss politics, poetry and loved ones
between bites of dried fish and rice cakes,
to hear the breathy notes of a wooden flute
and sip bitter green tea with Hanako
as cherry blossoms drift across the tearoom garden,
to watch the golden pink sunrise
spread high above Lake Kawaguchiko
from the summit of revered Mt. Fuji,
But
my words
cannot begin
to tell you
how it feels.

Grace Loving Gibson

Vaults

Grave mounds adorned with
    rows of great heart cockleshells
        pleated, flush-lined vaults.

edged with knobbed, creamy
    whorls of spiralled conches, shapes
        more intricately wrought

than carved stones
    with chiselled names and dates, than
        body's hidden bones,

mark what's left of man
    and mollusk, their goings, together
        land and sea wrack collected

here to lie under the
    vaulted coastal sky, rearranged
        in each other's praise.

Zan Gay

Leaving the Capitol at Sundown

For about seven seconds or a few moments or a minute and a half
I walked toward the monument
backlit by the peach glow of sunset,
thousands of pigeons and seagulls roosting in December trees,
taxis hooting as crowds emptied out from massive stone
buildings, I hailed a cab, stepped into it from the sidewalk,
asked for the Ritz,
and passed by a homeless fallen in his own vomit.

Howard Gordon French

Hunting at Weymouth

Blue steel clouds
touch Southern pine tops.
Dampness hangs
in the sweet air.
Weeping cherry trees
stand in the garden
of yesterday's hour.
Crisp leaves wet
from the morning
create a hunter's dream
to stalk the past.
The scent prevails
in darken hallways,
storeroom of words,
dream forging chambers
and where oak stokes smoke.
The stalker,
loaded with lead and paper,
stills breath on stand —
watches dust settle.

Grace B. Freeman

In the High School Locker Room

I bruised easily.
An incidental bump
against a chair and the mark
was there, purple and sinister.
I often hid behind long sleeves
until the color faded,
sometimes pretended
it was my monthly period --
the excuse my mother said
she used for skipping gym.

In the locker room that day
the girl dressing next to me
wanted to swap stories
about our healing wounds,
showed me her discolored upper arm,
explained almost proudly
her father beat her
only when he was drunk.

I was glad the bell rang when it did.
Would she have believed my tale
about the chair?
Would I have dared brag about
a gentle father who did not drink
except an eggnog at Christmas --
and coffee, black?

Virginia Fleming

Wind in the Grass

The wind in the grass
cannot be taken into the house
    The fragrance of a flower
    cannot be forever inspired.
    The song that the mockingbird
    sings through the dawn
    will not be written in notes
    that man has acquired...

and my feelings of love
cannot be told in a thousand words --
emotions grown so deep
spoken word could never arouse.
No tune has been written yet
with verve enough...and

    the wind in the grass
    cannot be taken into the house.

Lula Gay Fitzgerald

Handley Ridge

O luscious heaven!
   Pulled up from earth's brink
And held aloft by the
   finger of God,
   Shimmer;
Thy glory I would laud!

Sweet, leafless trees,
   Show forth thine ashen,
Tangled-limb balls
   Ornamental
Now there is no fall.

And merry children
   Clap hands for glee!
Romp and shout and play
   I rejoice with thee!

Heaven, trees, children,
   Handley Ridge
   of thee I recall these.

Robert J. Evans

Echo in an Empty Shell

That day, you stood upon the wind-swept beach,
watching the wild waves curling up in a frothy foam,
seeing the surging surf beating upon the shore.
You turned to me and smiled; A smile that was
far more radiant than the bright sun above us.
Your lips moved, but the wind snatched your words
so I could not hear what you were saying,
but I could tell it was a moment filled with meaning.

Today I held a seashell to my ear
and I could hear the ocean's roar.
I strained to hear your voice
from that day long vanished from this scene.
Can hearts speak to each other
without the sound of words or voice?
If so, my heart now echoes in return
because the seashell said, "I love you!"

Elon G. Eidenier

Wildacres, NC

Clouds graze
each ridge
leave each peak
silent in wool.
We collect
paper, ink,
language becomes
landscape-
the effervescence
of bone.
A hawk
dots space
geometric point
quantum leap
of flight.
Trees, green
upon green,
light glances
always to shadow.
We, by imagination's
force
craft words
in the belief
they might
catch currents-
soar,
hook beaked
to strike
the heart
like a hawk.

Robert Du Meer

Exploration

We explored whole
continents, oceans
found stone-age
people in our century,
examined brains
replaced pumps
repaired short circuits
made whole bodies.

Marvellous, aren't we?

A bird flew
through the window
Funny
All I saw was glass.

Lucile Noell Dula

Automatic Transmission

Hocus-pocus, little car
How I wonder where you are?
Parked within this mammoth lot,
Honk, so I can find the spot.

Irene Dayton

The Blackbird's Wing

In old courtyards
water weeps   on stone
where rocks and trees
enfold memories
for the living.
When night's chill
opens up a world
of knowing
we abandon ourselves
in search   of meteors
run of stars
until we look upon
sun rising
the blackbird flying.
From that wellspring
of light   dreams fall away
into a wild exuberance
of another seeing-
water on stone   rays of sun
revealing
memorial gardens for war's dead.

Vida B. Howard Cole

The Mad Pithoculopian Tree

In the all-green front yards where the East wind blows,
singing through the car-port spaces
Tell me, is it the Mad Pithoculopian Tree?
The tree, which rattles in the night scattering curly pods
with windy crazies and whining:
Tell me, is it the Mad Pithoculopian Tree
that shakes its tiny leaves so green,
raising high the pods of black, white and silver?

In the green fields where fairies dance,
they wave their skirts and blouses in the wind,
the edge circles their dreams.
Tell me: Is it the Mad Pithoculopian Tree?
Without help, the fairies put pods into their baskets
to shell out for beads.
Tell me: Is it the Mad Pithoculopian Tree
which strings beads for the Fairy Princess?

The fairies adorn themselves with seven kinds of beads.
The beads sparkle with a thousand brilliant prisms.
Tell me: Is it the Mad Pithoculopian Tree
which grabs the mane of the unicorn?
Never sad, never complaining.
Tell me: Is it the Mad Pithoculopian Tree
which calls for new dreams coming?
Now tell me: Is it the Mad Pithoculopian Tree waving to me?
Waving a scarf of lacy leaves.

The unicorn trotted under the Mad Pithoculopian Tree.
The fairies decorated the horn with strands of beads.
Their baskets spill seeds for more beads to hang on the unicorn.
The Mad Pithoculopian Tree kept shaking its branches.
The fairies opened their dreams
about the giving and giving,
of the Mad Pithoculopian Tree.

Brunice C. Cole, Jr.

Invitation to Break

Leave your typing, come with me.
I wait where the garden
is prettiest, by the fountain

where the concrete fish
spews torrents of water,
and cold streams

mumur between the apple
trees, where red roses
bloom, and quivering petals

fall. In the meadows
the bay horses roam
among spring flowers

which scent the air.
Stir the grape's nectar.
Fill our gold cups with love.

G. F. Caywood

Mt. Rainier Meadows

I went for a walk through the meadows
again today.
Up to where the glaciers begin,
and I followed the trails
    along the ice-line,
        and found the secret places
            where the wildflowers hide
                under the snow.
It was a little foggy, as it is always
a little foggy,
    but the walk was exhilarating,
        this, my last liberation
            among the wild flowers,
                until I return to this
                    place again.
I allowed myself a little more time,
    this time, to observe more closely
        the beauty of the meadows.
            In nature, there is never
                enough time to appreciate
                    all of it.
I will miss this place,
    the marbled brooks,
        the natural gardens
            the passions I have developed
                for all this wonder.
But, I will return,
    and I know I risk
        the chance that it will not be
            as I remember,
                not the same,
                    but will be as beautiful.

Mary Belle Campbell

Pine Lake at Twilight

In the afterglow of February sundown
two migrating ducks overfly our house --
fore-flyers of the flocks to come.

They swoop down over the pine-rimmed lake,
land on water, join the wintering
mallards, the pintails and widgeons
feeding here on the corn we spread
at water's edge.

The air tonight is soft as the lapping
water, sweet with songs of indefinable
pre-spring waking, quiet as the maples
lining the inlet to the lake, their branches
reddening, swelling to liven
with starbursts of strange red-brown tree
flowers. Something of last year's dying
is in the air, swelling to ripen anew.

Even as we do. We go from one year,
one love, one life, to another,
knowing spring will unfold us,
summer fly us, autumn flay us,
till our veins burst with longing
to understand, and we drop down
to lie with mosses and fungi under layers
of leaves, flexing our muscles on stone.

Lynda Calabrese

Geodes

We walk along the dry wash,
Tapestry Cliffs close
streaked pink and black,
an obvious inspiration
for designs on ancient pottery.

With canteens weighing us down
in one hundred degree heat
we talk about the lazy Rangers
who let the river
blaze their trails.

Even I climb into holes
sculpted by the river's run.
We give our names to arches
we barely fit into.

Looking for geodes,
the kids crack open river-strewn nodules,
hoping for jewels
in this echoed space

while we take roll after roll of film
as if we could keep the day
like a stone.

Sally Buckner

Traffic

Leaving the driveway, devising an easy cruise,
on flawless surface we move with facile grace
towards our anticipated rendezvous.

Serenely weaving through neighborhood avenues,
beneath the arbor limbs of elm enlace,
we drive more surely, savor this easy cruise.

On country highways, we react to cues --
broad vistas, open lanes -- increase our pace,
for we must keep our cherished rendezvous.

On freeways, we, like startled kangaroos,
leap swiftly forth into the frantic race.
What happened to our dream of an easy cruise?

In the city's heart, we grasp at each excuse
to dominate the road, command the chase,
and, yes, move forward towards our rendezvous--

if we can recall the address. We question the crew,
but no one remembers; we haven't a clue or a trace.
Forever ago, we began an easy cruise
towards what must have been an important rendezvous.

Sandra Z. Bruney

Searching for Arrowheads After Plowing

Newly turned, the earth seems stunned
at its exposure, shrinking from the sun's
burning eye. Clods of dirt crumble
beneath the brightness of that searing gaze.
The flint's scalloped edge gleams
where the plow has scraped it clean:
an alien shape rescued from the roundness
of the stones, the earth, the sun.

The arrowhead summons a vision
of the patient artist
who shaped his splintered bits of rock
by chipping away at the fragile edges,
wetting them with droplets of water,
(sighing perhaps at the ache in his bent back)
binding them with deer-gut thongs to a peeled shaft,
fire-hardened,
to make a child's first arrow,
or a warrior's spear.

One shaft must have missed its mark
and burrowed itself into leaf-rich loam until,
time-cleansed of all but its essential shape,
it sank through the waiting earth
like a shell drifting slowly downward
through a bottomless sea.

Artist, hunter, and prey, all silent
as the voiceless song of the vanquished forest,
until the iron prow split the waiting field apart
and spewed in its plodding wake
their mute and ancient epitaph.

Eloise Brock

Enigma of a Mountain

Did my colossal mass
of bouldered ore
push slowly, steadily
above the crust?
Or did I burst upright
screaming from uterinic thrust
as I tore the pelvic earth?

Was layer upon layer of my inner
core forced to rise, leaving me
bare and indecent,
crimped as easily
as a lock of hair,
until the grinding roar
wasted to exhaustion?

The ages draw a veil.

Peter Bougades

The Same Seat

It's just a way
Beyond the city limits
Where brim and bass do bed
And I go
In all seasons
To fish and watch the shore.

For in my boat
Above the water
The pictures are never the same
Except the sun
And the pier
Change is constant.

And that is tradition
And that is lore
To see with one's eye
Where new colors are born
And thickets grow
And a robin reappears.

For by the light
Of the sun
A man may still be free
To travel miles within a mile
And never change his seat.

Betsy Bostian

Wings of an Angel

It's a joy for a New Englander
to find a church down South
that doesn't need a bucket of white paint
splashed on the inside.
Most Southern churches are dark as
the tombs they are leading us to.

So, I enter the service to have my indrawn breath
turn white as the walls, the pews, the altar.
The minister stands there in white robe and stole,
his hair silver white as a saint's.

After white cells gave up fighting,
wife, mother, friend left the white sheets
of a hospital and took flight
on the vapor trail of a ghost plane.

Mourners are white as
the leukocytes that killed her.
Tears, diamond white, glisten in the eyes
of the woman minister friend.

But, we sing van Dyke's <u>Hymn of Joy</u>
and "drive the dark of doubt away"
with sun and stars, the light of day,
with white on white.

Elizabeth Bolton

Ave Maria

As I sit in church
head bowed, weary,
distressed by many cares,
the sounds of Ave Maria
pour from the organ.
The music envelops me,
flows into me.
I rise with it,
float through stained glass windows,
fly up and up
until I break against the sky.
Shattered pieces of me
hang in the upper air.
A part of me
is a part of the wind.
I rustle the leaves of many trees,
blow fiercely in a storm.
I drift in a summer cloud,
fall as water
to quench a parched field.
A drop in a mighty river,
I flow finally into the sea.
At peace,
I feel calm, serene,
beyond understanding.

Lee P. Arnold

Hanger

Bare hangers stare from the closet
Where you stood
To choose each day.
They gnarl and twist
Together at the ends
That hook.
Some hang forlorn,
Bereft of shirt,
Awry and desolate.
Some escape
The four-walled bias;
While wire bent by paroxysm
Finds no escape.
On tender hooks
They wait
To serve.

Nancy H. Banks

Cycle

In green porchrockers
we face the sound,
remembering other Augusts
when mosquitoes reigned.
Young lovers rocked
to tunes on wings,
planning life together.
Then children romped
on wide front porch
and rocked with mates.
Now babies climb
on green porchrockers
and face the sound
while mosquitoes reign.

Kate Dunn Barrow

Anzio Remembered

The beach was mined
And still the sun shone through the mists
As tides poured in on scheduled time
And blue waves rose to majestic heights
Before they curled in ruffled disdain
Of battles pitched in Power's name.

The tide will scour the beaches clean
The sea will render bombs inert
And children as in ages past
Will roam the shore
Seeking shells as museum pieces
While growing strong in nature's light
To transcend Might with Right.

Joseph Bathanti

Burn Season

"God talks in the trees."
--Thomas Merton <u>The Sign of Jonas</u>

All day chainsaws
ring us and rave their litany
of cut
and cut. There can be no
tomorrow. It is five o'clock
and already the icy moon is tethered
above the church of Mt. Zion.
We see it from our bedroom.
Its white spike steeple points
toward heaven. Its clapboard
walls are like snow, much with us -
a winter Purgatory.
Smoke fills the house with musk.
Ants spill from the wood
at the first trickle of flame.
Beneath the buckling bark,
grubs and glowworms disintegrate.
Forget that dirt is the last refuge.
In the split pit of wood so sharp
it sparked at the maul, I have found
chain, barbed wire, a hatchet head;
even a swatch of calico, a coffin nail,
and a small bone. We live in
the trees, without knowing;
we live in the fire.

Susan Block

The Eastern Edge of Tight

Looking at toes splayed
out like palm fronds,
the result of an invention
called the flip flop,
I long to see a
good old fashioned sandal
on a young foot.

The best are the kind
with wide white
leather straps that go
over a little girl's toes,
back to the sole
and then are buckled softly into
place around a pink heel
by a mother who smells like
shampoo and soap.

Once past the squeaky door,
the lines do fall in pleasant
places for a child
wearing sandals
fastened just on the
eastern edge of tight.

Ron Bayes

The Burning of the Imperial Cafe on Depot Street

Not only did the joke of a down-town
sociological center where the old whore
house was go up in smoke so

did a lot of other dreams and wild drunks
at breakfast and other dreams and the
assuagement of coffee and the necessity of

checks cashed and the plural necessities
of cheap meals; a great deal indeed of what
there was in my town went—went with the enjambment

of the reality, a harsh reality. Pasts and dreams
sent out to hope to find a new joint
to feel pretty much at home in any time,

any time of day or any day. The cigar
store went up in the same flames—over a quarter
of a city block. Worst of all the shock again

in the peculiar center of the chest, shock
telling again, "You can't stop time."
It took four hours to be able
to go to the scene with others.

Margerie Goggin Allen

Two Roses

The larger rose explodes in petals
and splays its flaming essence
across a morning-dared meadow,

red and robust as a proud banner
murderously furled
in the blood of a killing field,

down under the dead boy who held it
amid time-honored lies
on both sides fighting the battle.

The smaller rose unfolds slowly
in the morning-taut energy
of dew-wet petals,

manufacturing its mauve fables
of a lady-in-waiting
from an ancient kingdom

who was traded
for eight black Arabian stallions
and forty pieces of silver

As she carried the proud banner
of her grieved obedience,
unfolding morosely to a rough husband

unschooled in the nectar-blest,
honey-touched, unction
of love.

Marsha Warren

Early February

*People wonder how birds find their
way 12,000 miles, why swallows return
to Capistrano the same day each year.*

The only light in Surf City blinks red and yellow and
Positively No Credit Cards is taped to the town's only pump.
In driving snow, "Rooms for Rent" slaps loud against the
WORMS & TACKLE SHOP. Turtle's Inn Cottages, abandoned,
empty shells, scatter peeling paint on a yard gone wild,
like a bird whose photoperiodism jammed, I come to this beach
in winter.

Pale skin, muffler-drawn, rubber boots through grasses
not trusted in June, I migrate for renewal to the water's edge,
its summer sun and salt. The sea in slow-motion discards shivering
froth in the sand where shells lay dead and clothespins hibernate
with drooping lines and icicles on boarded cottage porches.
Brown seaoat stalks I never pick green, break hollow in my hand.
Out of place, a single clutch of daffodils bends wildly to the wind
on my return path. In mittened hands I grab them up, escape to my
room beside the grill that's "Closed till Spring."

*Turtles migrate 14,000 miles from
Brazilian waters to Ascension Island,
their migration triggered by the length
of the day.*

Time

The Summer Land....

Kay Nelson

Weeds of Time

She remembered the tree,
pink blossoms fell that summer day.
Flower by flower,
the pieces of her life,
rested on the soft earth,
dropped into the darkened holes.

She found the grave stones,
flat rectangles against cold ground.
Brushing aside years of growth,
she traced, "Infant son of...,
Husband of... ."

The tree had grown,
long branches sway
in the cool morning breeze,
like a man's arms wanting,
a child's needing.

She pulled the weeds of time,
crushed them between her fingers,
gathered pink blossoms from
the tree, and left her footprints,
walking through the cemetery.

Margaret B. Baddour

Birthday Revolution, January 2

Here at the coming round,
where my own year bumps
the new year, I have found
my mind's sharp sphere.

And my body, summer severed,
still tasting mangoes,
stretches enough sunward
to last from cold to cold.

Tousled, both body and brain,
by the climb, only I appear
clutching at the chain
that holds my wayward moon.

His twisted laughter
and the tendency to spin
keep me turning, chasing after
little stars that always fall.

Judy Goldman

Last Night

It was late enough to see a luna moth.
From where I stood I could watch
it wave, such quick flicks of wing
you'd think the moon was pulling strings,
knuckling that small body
as if it were the immaculate hand of a magician
turning a silk scarf into gardenias,
into something that flies,
into a daughter old enough to move so far away
her mother can only stand in the unmowed grass
watching the sky, the one thing left
they have in common.

Marie Gilbert

Spider Fall

Sheer spun is the thread holding
our individual spider dangling
swaying - our deadly spider

venom tailored to chill our special blood,
legs at length to fit the shoulders
tighten the throat, still the pounding heart.

Skipping along beneath the trees
open arms embracing what comes
no need to strain deciphering marks on tummies

of spiders swinging in gossamer suspension
from branches turning winter bare.
When leaves slip, catch each bright finality

with your eyes if not with your hands,
the spider that drops, will fall
when spiders will.

Nancy Bradberry

Alone

Tonight I saw the first firefly.
One small light
where last summer
we watched so many.

A treat for you
to stay up late to see
magic in our yard.
You laughed, were happy.

You loved those lights
flashing in the dark.
Not to be caught, captured,
trapped, but flying free.

And now I watch
that same remembered signal
wink in the darkness
of my life alone.

Juanita Dawson

Forecast

This snow light morning
sleet threw a blanket
like a housekeeper bound
to cover beds and birds.
Surprised, the daffodil
foliage sleeps prostrate.
Ice buds on trees
shrubs, a glass scene.

On newspaper watch
Dinah Shore
and her Holly Farms type
pop up timer
starts furnace air
nudging the curtains.

We bet our thermometers
against the forecasters'
absorb their layered advice
play checkers with words
get hypothermia handwriting.

Climax to no snow pudding
true to wonderland
folded daffodils spring back
as evening slips beneath
rippled wool of dark.

Dede Wilson

Saying it Out Loud

Somewhere
a woman bends
without remorse,
she may be dancing,
or reaches
for dangling fruit
or a cup on a shelf

with no remininiscence.
Somewhere someone
does not bite
the ragged corner
of her day
at dawn

and suck on the bitterness.

When you come to me
in your patience
and your silence
and say
you never think about it,

I begin to see.
In this fine sequence
of conciliation,
forgiving life for now,
its weaving in and out
of shadow, I find

you are bearable.

Ellen Harrington Weisiger

Wisteria

Untended, you cling
   to my house for your life
      with serpentine arms.
Your lavender-purple
      panicles of fragrance
         slight as innocence,
intoxicate, deceive me.
         Nights, I hear you gallop
      like race horses
round my doors and windows
      to bind me in ropes,
         uproot the foundation.
In swords of moonlight
      I grope in the basement,
         grasp the loppers,
crop my way out.
      With an axe
         I chop your vital trunk.

Breathless, I lie in tall grass
      doors unlocked
         windows open.

Hazel Foster Thomas

Eye Has Not Seen

Many times
 I visualize God, and
all his wonder.
Grown older,
Heaven seems closer.
I yearn to see, and
embrace loved ones
beyond the veil.
When I gaze at sailing clouds
I feel helpless as a prisoner;
who flattens his hand
against the glass;
that separates him
from his only visitor.

Jane Kirkman Smith

Images In Transit

Let me tell you how it rose this time -- although
when I cannot say. Did some almanac maker
determine an average time?

As short as I am, I should live west of my
weekends -- as I live east of work -- I say to myself
because the sun takes aim for my eyes early Friday
afternoon and for a long time Monday morning.
I squint out from under my clam shell of a visor
and skim along slightly beneath the sky. The blue
serrated edge of the horizon all around seems to
lift me and bear me along above the highway below.
I had looked forward to seeing the sunrise
early this Monday but hadn't bargained for this.
Five sunsets in one day had impressed John Glenn
I know, but had he ever zipped through the
Carolina mountains this time of day.
The late October valley had still been in shadow
when I left; then my brain was pierced
with sunlight when I moved from
behind the first peak and then the next.
Then it happens -- flash -- flash and I am
blinded by sunrise after brilliant sunrise,
white spokes penetrating the mist.
Russet, scarlet, gold and wine
strobe in and out of focus again -- again -- again.

E. Carrington Smith

Play the Tune

Play the tune
Sing the song
Do you remember?
Has it been too long?
Round and Round
One, two, three
Summer's sounds
In Memory.

Morning's brand new
Nature glistening with diamonds of dew
Birds chirping
Butterflies flitting, flirting
Bees humming
Buds blooming
The old gray cat on the porch
lazily grooming.

Grass growing sweet
'Neath light, carefree feet,
Little boys frolic and scamper,
Dogs romping after.

Play the tune
Now do you remember?
When life was fresh and tender
And you were young and free.

D. L. Smith

And I

And I, attached as it were, to a droplet
And sitting prismatically on the edge of the world.
My feet soled with objectivity
But my heart writhing in pain as intellect feels for calm.
Am I the sole possessor of reason I ask or nearly as strong
as the balance fulcrum seeking always the perfect balance?

Master, I think, of reality
Finding myself in the midst thereof.
For every leaf that falls one freshly unfolds or else I have
no surety that my last breath taken in will let out again.
Going is restless without thinking of the return: cliff's
edge is someone someplace else.

I find myself stepping cautiously,
As if going someplace important forever.
"Ask the purple moth," instructs the night,
"why she flies in silent wisdom. She knows
more than you. She seeks one more day only.
Caress the candle wax and wonder that she
gives all for you. Your thoughts ride on her
flame."
"Tonight the moth and the flame choose counsel
with you. There is no sacrifice. There is no equation."

Bertie Reece Smith

The Breeze

There is nothing
Softer
Than a breeze
Whose fingertips
Dance across my face
And stroke my hair,
With exquisite gentleness,
Into tendrils
And smooths the tired
Pain of anxiety
From my thoughts
In heat of summer.
This is as close to
Heaven
One can get.

Are there breezes in
Heaven?
There must be...
Angels have wings.

Sally W. Smisson

Persephone

Black is for her winter throne
Where she sits silent
Till distant robins fly and Cerberus
Growls low but lets her trade
her twilight gray for Demeter's
sun-splashed, new-grass green.

Marty L. Silverthorne

Silence that Separates Them

Tonight they are not quarreling over cover,
pulling blankets and quilts handed down
mended with generations of blind stitches.

Tonight they rest seperate side by side under
a quilt of clay covered with wiregrass,
the same grass their children flat hoed.

Tonight they are not quarreling over
work money he spent on whiskey or women
she heard rumored he slipped 'round with.

Tonight he does not bicker or bitch about
indoor plumbing or how the Kennedys ruined
everything Lincoln set free.

Tonight they are not arguing over
Cronkite's wax-lipped newscast.
She is not humming through the hymnal.

Tonight he is not swelling her with child,
filling her with fear of stillborn. Tonight
they are resting under a red quilt
with a silver satin lining, wrapped
in their Sunday meeting specials,
tobacco money duds.

Randolph P. Shaffner

Elixir

So how could I have known within a week
That I would cherish you for fifty years?
When age has bleached the flush of passion's cheek,
The incandescent blaze of love appears.
Should son or grandson seek from me advice
On how to know when love has come his way
For sure, could I advise -- will it suffice
To say -- I loved you by the seventh day?
When earth forgot to blink at the moon's pearled white
And moon beheld in wonder earth's swirled blue,
Did earth or moon regard the eye at night
That predetermined they would rendezvous?
My heart full fifty years before my mind
Knew what I now know fifty years behind.

Ruby Shackleford

Found Poems-I

That bird singing
effects the flow
of fancy. It lifts
a nourishing draught
to flagging sense.

In this trill
Is the leaven of wildness
    medicative to the spirit.

I long for wildness,
forever unproved.

I would go to the hills
for strength,
would match the fate
of Alcestis.
The fairest of the wood
is the exhiliration
of the cardinal
the mediator between
my housed barbarism and his untenanted peace.

JR Seed

Nights' Stage

Cedar wisps
paint by moonglow,
white lace
on night's face.
While in concert,
bird song,
accompanied by
wood winds
and wind chimes,
is punctuated by
owl's call.
As oaks sway
to earth's beat
and stretch
in majestic applause.

Rebecca Schenck

Pretend a Seance

Turn the white globe low
till light is a lavender scene
on the shade of a Tiffany lamp.
Uncle Clyde, come in the kitchen,
wearing the grocer's apron
your father asked you not to wear.
Stand beside the butcher's block
worn deep along one edge
and look at me through rusty tongs
that used to hook a hundred pounds of ice
when the sign was in the window.

Could we go out to Ponder Lake,
feed the fish our scraps from supper?
I think about you in September;
you're the only one who had
a birthday close to mine.
I found the butter mold in the barn,
saved framed certificates to show
you and your sisters recited catechisms.
What should I do with them now?
In the box of things of yours
is a photograph of me.

Rebecca Ball Rust

Haiku Sequence

end of the old pier,
a dead flounder's eye stares
at the autumn moon

cold mist on the sea,
smoke pours from the mouths of fish
cooking on the fire

rising moon,
in the fish-cleaning sink
the sparkle of scales

rain pool,
mosquito flies away
from itself

dawn...
a broken cane chair sits
facing the ocean

Alba T. Kern

Life's Senses

He could not see the sky, the sun -
 The daylight beauties surrounding him...
He could not see the stars at night,
 The moon which shines in all its splendor.
He could not hear bluebirds that fly,
 Singing as though they had not a care.
 He could not see the rose blooming,
 Nor hear brooks and streams, sounds they render.
He could not feel the gentle breeze,
 E'er brushing across his face and hands...
He could not feel the tingle of rain,
 Prancing to and fro, falling on him...
He could not taste the salted sprays,
 The sea gives out with whip-splashing waves.
He could not taste, nor see, hear, feel --
 Too busy - such waste - life's light - too dim.

John M. Marshall

The Night's Mare

Breaking through the clouds at the speed of light:
Starry-hoofed, comet-crowned queen of night.
Fire-breathing dragonfly, how she rushes by
Windows of the soul in the midst of flight!

Lightning flashes from her gossamer wings.
Thunderous sounds from her feet she flings.
Star-stream voyager, brighter than a meteor,
Swiftly 'round the moon's pale sickle she swings.

Knocking at the door of secret dreams,
Ecstasies of childhood she fervently redeems.
Running like a whirlwind, hastening the night's end,
Magically she fades into dawn's gold beams.

Caroline Rowe Martens

On Sunday

I shake the heavy linen cloth and
send crumbs tumbling into the mid-day
wind; they spin 'til gravity dips them
down and greater ground assumes the role
of host. Most, if not all, will be gone
by dark; gleaners will clean them away;
no spark of recall will haunt the spot.
Short is the half-life of ritual.

Eleanor Rodman May

Going to the Highway Patrol Station

After the three o'clock bell has thrown
freedom into November's air,
It is I, not she who lingers
in the crowd outside the swinging doors.

Inside the station
halls flow with figures of authority
and gush with guys, sixteen, in jeans,
who smell of smoke, swing new car keys.
Future drivers park themselves
in chairs, watching each other
like dogs prepared to fight.

Near the Examiner's desk, a bulletin board
begs, "Say No To Drugs"
and, "If You Drink, Don't Drive."
Above my daughter's head these words
pile up like leaves.

Small figure that follows a uniform,
twig she pulls and breaks from me.
Then drives away
unafraid of anything, guilty of innocence,
gone.

Mary Coe Mears

Richness of Spring

The delta green smells of fresh earth
   tucked under slant-banked rills.
Jasmine fragrance penetrates warm, wind-swept
   evening air.
Chestnut ponytail swings gently; a heart races
   wildly to full-moon stirrings
As nature, mysterious and wonderful, sends
   goose-bump shivers along the spine ---
Wonderful richness of spring!

Susan Meyers

Breakfast Gathering

One woman says her suns rise
ripe for danger,
morning murders over coffee.
She wears walking shoes
to track the hours
slipping down the hall.
But come sundown,
her nights are old movies
of someone else's days.
She has willed them to the stars.

She says how hard September strives
for balance,
with sycamores giving up green.
Beyond the window
sometimes a deer, glimpsed at dawn.
Today an embarrassment
of tobacco stalks,
stripped to brown and yellow.

Near the B-wing entrance
lost vines wonder
how to creep down trees
to winter.
It has come to this:
   the biscuit beige
   of roadside weeds.

Soon sun will lose its hold,
will yield to moon
the close watch over fields.
The woman smiles
at thoughts of winter.
She has learned to step
into the missing light.

Margaret Murray

Along the Path Today

Bone-white the carcass
Beside the path
No outline of flesh and hair
All the juices gone
Life reduced to sharp bones
Eyeholes like frozen zeroes
In the gnarled head
No Yorick or court jester here
But a beast who ate the summer grass
Who roamed through blooming pastures
Down to the streams
For thirsty gulps of water
Who called across the woods
To a mate in rut.
Don't tell me of war and death.
I met them along the path today.

Frances Outhwaite

To Keep

At sunset
the entire sky-bowl is washed
in rosy pink and purple. Crimson
jetstreams pierce the heavens
like lances. A pearly half moon
sits overhead.

Showy Jupiter,
his moons aligning themselves
in my telescope,
sparkles in the southeast.

I want to keep this moment,
mark it forever
on my inner eye.

Diana Pinckney

When Summer Comes

I will drop the wool of time,
throw screens to the ground,
call out to willows,
wear morning sun in my hair,

drive a silver convertible
in green smelling rain,
splash steaming
through gold washed afternoons.

At dusk in summer,
I'll drift with soft voices,
whisper secrets in a hammock
as shadows drape the air.

Nights will find me dancing
in a wooden pavilion over the marsh
where fiddler crabs hiss and click
in throbbing pluff mud.

Summer dawn will streak light
across my bed, show scattered poems
titled "Remember When"
I may mail to old loves.

I want to swing bare feet
to bare floors, slip
a cotton shift over my head, feel
it skim my body like a breath.

When summer comes, I'll allow
the leap of hope, believe
your lovely lies, and ride
the waves with you again.

Sam Ragan

Winter Lightning

It was into the third day
Of winter, the last of December,
I was awakened by the rumble
Of thunder, the wind rising,
And a cramp in my leg.
I sat in a darkened room
And rubbed away the cramp
While watching the lightning
Flash across the skies
Before the rains came.
I thought about last summer
When the storm was much the same
But the rain was longer
Than it is now,
With the lightning lighting up
The entire room, brighter than then.

Billie C. Huling

Thistle Down

The vacant lot was littered with cans,
    but weeds obscured the trash.
A blue-eyed toddler looked over the fence
    and spied the beauty there.
The tendril spikes of purple silk
    perched inside cups of green
    first caught her quick and sensitive eye
    as she teetered on her fence.

The summer flew by and ripened the seeds.
    The shimmering wind caught up their silk,
    wafting away on wings of down
    to the rich bottom land just east of town.
She cupped her hand to catch the sprites
    but grasped the thorns instead.
With a shock she learned how pain is hidden
    in the beautiful summer of life
    encased in a heavenly magic stalk.

Charron Pitts Hearn

The Soul's Seasons

Spring, the secret saint, nods in accord
As the wayfaring breeze hurries past,
Leaving promises on petals.

Summer, nature's pilgrim,
Creates shrines of sunshine and showers,
Doing penance in fragrance.

Fall -- a solemn, eloquent whisper --
Stands almost mute before Winter's onslaught,
Camouflaging death in color.

Winter, the eternal wanderer,
Bears God's frost like Cain,
Seeking the redemption of Spring.

The Seasons' guest enters the Wicket Gate --
        the garden gate --
To find the answers to unformed questions
        on a wing or in a fragrance.

Amid life's cacaphony he seeks solitude,
Sequesters his soul within the breeze,
Listens to the somber sound of doves,
And takes flight on whistling wings.

Always, there is a symphony of sound
        a feast of sight,
                and a respite from himself.

Frances W. Harrell

Our Last Autumn

I remember the soft, warm sun
On our backs
As we sat close together
In the old swing
That he had patched and patched.

One by one the sycamore leaves
Floated to the ground,
Each with its own silent sound
Of death and the promise of
Another spring.

I think we both knew
It was our last
Autumn together.

Lucille Griffin

Tomorrow

Fingers, wee and small
    reaching out to find the world.

Long, slender fingers
    balancing pencils, marbles, life

    now wrinkled and gnarled
reaching out for another day - tomorrow

Veta E. Gorman

Holographs

Two generations ago, sun-bleached shells
Made stories for children's vacations,
Shell chronicles, lost, transparent memories.
But, in those Great Depression days
She told us sand was silica, kin to fine crystal,
And that a special shell, named Strombus,
Was a Siamese princess,
Robe flung back, undressing.
She liked our giggles.
They didn't cost much.

I remember her now, with my collection:
Shells, once-living homes of animals, long dead,
And the bi-valves that were fine china,
Inlaid mother-of-pearl, for sea castles.
The gravelly shell particles were crowded faces,
But, I think of shell concrete, making houses,
For the homeless of the thirties
Or the nineties.

This conch could sing of a new deal
In brave baritone, or broken jargon
When encrusted with barnacles
Like public housing or camouflage
When the wars come.
Even this shy Scotch Bonnet,
Roll trimmed, pert plaid, saucy curl,
Seems too fragile a thing for hope.

All, all are blown, like outer banks,
Holographs of the sea.

Lynne Gause

The Vision

Some say my experience
came from the shadows
of the veil of death.
The dream, so vivid,
is with me still.
I was a laughing babe
in among hundreds,
with happy eyes.
Amid joyous sounds,
we waited to be born.
We swam in a stream
of uncaptured blue.
The water bubbled
as cherubs floated,
tasted, and breathed
the scents of Eden.

Nancy Gotter Gates

Flying Over Chicago at Night

As we fly swiftly eastward now I watch
the moving panorama of the earth
succumb to darkness well before its time.
The fields that stretch as far as I can see
in perfect squares of green and brown and tan
soon fade into obscurity as dusk
first softens, then obliterates their lines.
Now from the blackness unexpectantly
the first faint specks appear like flickering stars
that tumbled from the sky. And soon I find
they lie in perfect rows. The distant lights
have sprouted like the grain as though one night
some star-seed fell unnoticed onto earth
and settled into furrows men had plowed
for lesser crops. They grew and blossomed there
becoming geometric, incandescent
fields that set the sky ablaze for miles
with such celestial glow that I forget
how ordinary are the streets below.

Winnie E. Fitzpatrick

A Backward Glance

The wayward winds of time divide us now
From fading years of many decades past.
The thought of times we shared -- Remember how
The playing children seemed to grow so fast?
We poured out hearts together -- right or wrong
The secrets families can never know.
And as our children grew both tall and strong,
Warm thoughts filled parted years with afterglow.
And can it be, I hear your thoughts, you mine?
Now as my grown boys argue I reflect
The joys we shared among a friendly vine.
Recalling happy thoughts, I can't forget.
Alone, we'll walk the path ... Its final bend.
But I'll remember you ... A Love ... A Friend.

Kitty Beasley Edwards

Remembrance

Ah, was I ever, then, so young that each
careless dawn spewed pearls of time floating
free as iridescent eggs of salamander,
and yet impatience brought the naked feet
to pace and pace the night-damp shore...
sand seductively, insistently caressing...
while the fat old orange grinning moon
flowed his mellow molten gold across the
crests of dreamless Chinese soldier waves
marching forever on and on and on;
'til they danced, those traitorous feet,
foolish as panicked October leaves,
to tryst with sorcerer unburdened by
fidelity to promises given or received,
whose potent presence mortared over
the brain of she who had needed no one...
only culture, knowledge...had quested
through the painfully recorded lore
of centuries...around the earth
and even to the unimaginable heavens...
for truth and understanding;
and never, for a moment, thought to know
the searing, white-hot pain of mindless,
screaming, unrequited love?

Jeanie Estella Dragoo

Summer's Early Rise

Summer's early rise
Dressed and running down the path
To Grandmother's hug.

Raymond Dotson

Last Summer's Glove

There's my missing glove -
    fingers gone,
rotted away by last winter's
snow blanket drippings.
Small strands of Cotton drill
held together by polyester stitches,
    but green!
Still green as when
I broke the soil cap
and stuck muscadine cuttings
    (Blessed with Rootone)
down beyond their first knuckle.

What distracted me
that I left so hurriedly...
rushed away with just one glove?
Was that the time a yellow-jacket
stung little Jeffrey's foot
and you said, like always,
    "Daddy'll fix it!"
Or was that the day
you felt the first siezures of labor?
    (She was born in March,
    so the time would have been right)

Or perhaps nothing monumental happened.
Perhaps I merely felt a stirring -
looked up to find you gone
on some small errand
and followed.

Mary Dezarn

The Gap

In our winter woods
tough, dry brown leaves
cling to scrawny
long-standing oaks,
daring frost and wind
to loose their grip -
not choosing to go gently.
And some few will linger
still, when April, knowing,
nudges, whispers...
      relinquish
to a generation
bright and green.

Mary Alice Countess

September

September melts and runs on the edge of summer
Like a pat of butter on a warm plate.
Nature goes soft,
Soft as forgotten apple orchards.
The sun is a bee that has stung itself out.
Sap sinks like the water in wells,
And leaves are limp.
Dawn mists are made of kitten fur.
Tepid rains gentle open the locked earth.
Skies look well-laundered.
That first hilltop where a breeze is stirring
Is September,
And we summer runners who gain it
Can pull in a fresh cooling breath.
That first hollow where green trees cluster
Is September,
And we who have been tramping August's scorched plain
Can throw ourselves down in the shade.
We lie on the floor of the forest
While our breathing steadies and slows.
Pale mushrooms pierce the leafmold
Around us.
Acorns mottled like onyx
Lie scattered here and there,
Gems from a fairy tale.
They are hard.
The rest of September
Is soft.

Alice Carver Cramer

Young Magus

Christmas wonder woke him early, early
drew him from the unfamiliar bed and down the stairs.
Only his grandmother in the kitchen
saw him (whose mode is running)
dream-drift soft and slow in the dawn twilight
to the tree.
With no word she plugged in the lights --
See! A rainbow of sparks breaks into bloom.
He sinks to his knees.

This is his golden once-only Christmas
of knowing not knowing
remembering...what?
in his shining structure of expectation
his Christmas wonder.

His grandfather comes now
stands with his grandmother at the kitchen door:
These two watching the child, oblivious, on his knees
lifting his face to the light
caught in the golden spell
of this imperishable moment.

Louise Pugh Corder

Cardinal Guest

There's no more welcome, winter guest
Than redbird with his vivid crest.
Resplendent gem in crystal snow,
He lights, puffs plumage up just so
To shield him from the frosty cold
And bring his viewers joy untold!
Observe him quietly, he won't mind.
He's seldom shy of humankind.
A scarlet bloom on frozen lace,
He lends to chill scene, summer's grace.
His blazing beauty fires the heart
With gratitude for living art.

Emily Exner Chi

Limits

After a two-day journey in a trailer,
Swaying on highways, bumping on back roads,
Watching where she's been, not where she's going,
The black mare sees the ramp in place and steps
Carefully down the unfamiliar metal
Onto the pasture grass. And now she's free.
She ignores the lush forage and takes off
Galloping till she comes to the farther fence,
And galloping back till she reaches the other end,
Mane and tail flying, hooves pounding,
Back and forth and back and forth in joy
At finally being free.
          But there are limits
To all freedom as she learned at last.
One morning she was found in the lane with a gate
around her neck, lifted from its hinges.
Brought to her knees, she was puzzled and angry;
Her equine brain can't fathom that freedom is finite,
And that even Pegasus, equipped with wings,
Was turned back on the slopes of Mount Olympus.

W. T. Boyd

The Song of the Pumpkin Fairy

Enchanted pumpkins bring delight
In joyful cause this hallowed night.
By wave of wand and spritely chant,
A fairy brings what science can't:
        "Pumpkin hearts I give a flame to;
        'Jack-o-lanterns' now I name you.
        Open up your shining faces,
        Light the paths to strange new
        places.
Sit on sills in darkened rooms,
And light the night for witches'
brooms;
And when the children trick or
treat,
Thrill them from your window
seat!"

Ednah Bethea Blalock

An Exhortation

Watch!
Watch the tired robin
Whose winter time
Has come too soon...

What bitter suet
Has he now consumed
On well appointed lawns
And studied aviary
Condominiums.

We have lost those in flight
to doom and innocent
immobility.

Long ago, and long
The lead bird hovered,
Sampled the quiet meadows,
Held liturgy
at pastel dawn,
Reconnoitered...Then
Pointed a new direction.

Now the distraught path
Leads to oblivion...
The clarion sounds
Are heard no more....

Keeper and brother
Of the birds—Look sharp,
For we may never—ever
Sing again.

Jane M. Berryman

Winter Lullaby

In February, starved for sun, the spirit died,
and people of Finlandia turned out the children.

They could not understand, these little ones,
unwrapped, unfastened. How could they,
whimpering at the needle winds that stitched them
back and front. The tiniest babies gasped,
weakly cried, and if they were alone
and sisterless, soon died.

The older children, wide-eyed and aware, knew
better than to waste their life on tears.
For they had seen it coming, seen the building,
heard angry talk, these older children in their
wisest time, the time of knowing just before
concealing time. They smelled the deep infection,
made their plans.

Deaf to the piteous cries of those whose motherlove
they felt deprived of, whose furtive pinchings
they'd sustained, and whispered threats;
they seized their favorites only, raced away.

The streets were thick that day with children
stuck by frozen tears to lamp posts,
starey-eyed and grey.
Forsaken children pounded, sobbing, on shut doors,
and soon were silent heaps of numbness
on the thresholds.
Under the gelid sky, lowering, lowering,
No one was left to cry.

February, when starved for sun the spirit died,
the people of Finlandia turned out the children.
And munching little cakes and sipping wine,
the faces flushed with warmth, and tearbright eyes,
they made their celebration at a polished table.

Katherine Russell Barnes

August Redefined

The last few days --
before a thousand feet
in rubber soles
thud the concrete --
are pitched high.
Packed like school lunches
designed to sate and save.

On beaches frenzied bodies
writhe like nests
of newborn moccasins.
The sun on water doubles
its revenge
and on the boardwalk
every carnival seat
is filled.

Mountains expand
push against belts
of car-covered roads
that bind, reshape.
Caves open their mouths
to mile-long lines
of instant Hedonists.

My hand
resting on the gearshift knob
is reflected in the window.
Fingers, like stalactites
developed from one drop
and over time
grew, stiffened,
stretched long from reaching.

James H. Banbury

Breakthrough

January's stiffly set, cold descends.
Bowed branches parry wind gusts, rains slash,
    sleet flings gravel, ice varnishes, snows erase.
Ignoring possibilities, daffodils appear,
    cover pushed aside.
Poor timing! Absurd and foolish!
February's frosts lie in wait,
    surges of subfreezing nights,
    days stonejacketed by season's press.
Seeming not to care, daffodils grow,
    buds swell, tips yellow.
Small heralds of spring hope
    that break the grip of winter.

George A. Wilcox

My Porch

My screened porch is like a tree house
Tall among the pines
Resting softly on cushions of dogwood.
Scattered below, the daffodil patches beckon.

Spring is heaven's gift
A return of life in lovely forms
My porch is front row center.
As nature's curtain unfolds
And the production begins
Framed by branches and leaves
Budding,
Dogwood, azaleas, and redbud
Bursting.
Add the melodic chorus
Of robins, cardinals, and wrens
And the theatre dances before me
And the audience applauds.

Mary Auman Adams

The Snowman's Passing

Yesterday you stood

>   tall and proud snowman
>   a backbone of hard packed snow
>   imprints of knitted mittens
>   in your middle bulge,

Today's sunlight reveals

>   the veins of life aren't in you
>   as your scarf soaks in the melted slush,
>   your hat remains cocked in its jaunty slide
>   over one coal eye,

>   your carrot nose drooping downward
>   and you'll soon drop your broom,

A cold statue of nature

>   with no life's warmth
>   portraying an old man with wounded pride
>   on his last stance of life,

Yet, the shiny gloss of melting snow

>   looks almost
>   as if sweat is on your brow,

But only a hard freeze can save you now!

People

Where the Weak Grow Strong and the Strong Grow Great....

Anthony S. Abbott

A Small Thing Like a Breath

How cheap words are. How easy to say,
"I love you," knowing not even the surface
of the word. How easy to say, "I'd die for you,"
knowing not even the icy edge of death, not even
his outer garments. Then you bear a child.

You carry a life in the darkness of your womb
for nine uneasy months. The child descends,
bumping the fragile edges of its unformed skull
against the walls of your pelvic bone. He enters
the world wailing. For a time the machines help
him breathe, and you cannot hold him because of
the wires, the sensors which mark each vital function.

So you give him your finger to grasp, and you gaze
at the miracle of his tiny, perfectly formed nails.
And after many hours you are still not tired,
not finished marvelling at the wonder you have
created, and you know that you could, indeed <u>would</u>
die for this son -- this beautiful, selfish, glorious,
heartbreaking son.

And every night you continue to marvel.
Every night before sleep you tiptoe into his room
and listen to each small breath and watch the way
he seems to smile. And later you will keep pictures,
you will mark his first step and the awkward rounded
shapes of his first letters. You will shout with joy
at his first line drive, and when he hurts you will

know the very marrow of love, how pain for his pain
takes you in its arms and grips like icy night.
Then, when you speak of love and death, you will do so
not lightly, but with bowed head and hushed respect
for a small thing like a breath.

Lois Holt

Signs

The night you leaned through the kitchen door,
your breath hotter than the open flame,
everything cooking tilted to the left
on those uneven eyes. Burned to a crisp
while you damned us all to Hell and back.

My mother was a believer in "signs",
her premonitions and predictions gospel
enough that when the picture of the lost lamb
slid slowly down the wall and rested upright,
glass unbroken, against the baseboard,
I came to know the meaning of her promise of salvation.

Taking this shortcut back to Georgia,
I pass long lines of mobile homes, shanties,
abandoned cars rusting on their axles.
The women are still there.
Wash drags the ground, pulls the poles to center.
Children draw circles in the mud.
I count old TVs, refrigerators, stoves
pitched through the open doors
leaning at wierd, cockeyed angles,
broken down and no good to anybody.

So much easier to throw out than a man.

Judith Holmes Settle

Looking for Morning

The old man walks beyond the plowed field,
through the green thicket and over the rise.
Eyes groundward, he follows a path
of memories locked inside.
In the curling shade of a weeping willow,
he kneels before a foot-high cross,
paces the yardstick-length of a grave.

He recalls the pressure of a wood coffin
shouldered uphill,
sun blaring on his face,
sweat and tears pouring across his mouth.

Today, he jerks a bandana
from his pocket, swipes his eyes,
hitches his left shoulder,
and stares into the sun.

He retraces his steps,
stumbles in the back door.
"Where've you been?
I've been worried sick," she scolds.
"You know you're not supposed to be out alone."

He sits, stares into the fire.
"I walked across the woods," he mumbles,
"looking for the morning."

Shelby Stephenson

Lee Terry

Stopped at the barn
just long enough to let me
know he was not
going to climb the tierpoles:
looked like a treetrunk
standing in the door:
turtle-shell, dome-shaped
hard hat:

tightened lips:
      he'd stand there on the sandy bottom of the barn,
never speaking:
three men -- one on the top rack of tiers, one
below, and Lee on the ground
in his cut-off shirt, that right arm like a hog's ham
his nostrils flaring: poking the bulky stick of green tobacco
up to the man on the lower tierpoles:

a look of pure displacement
as if the sky were a roof-dome
and the dirt beneath his feet
might move mountains.

Mary Louise Medley

Honda Boy

He's roaring down the asphalt ways
These gilded, haunting autumn days.
A proud young god of jet dream speed,
Whose gleaming Honda laps with greed
The miles that make a thrilling whirl,
Which he now shares with his Honda girl.
She clings behind him unaware
That life and death are just a dare,
And nothing much holds in between
Save two gay helmets, red and green.

Marie Kennedy Robins

Gospel

The blue-haired woman under the hot helmet
at Golden Shear Beauty Shoppe remembers
how once she wanted a pond with an island
of her own and a tiny bridge going to it.
Fred started a fishing pole business.
Now an imprisoning bamboo forest
chides the hubcap sculptures,
forever stunts the idea of a lake.

Lawyer Wingo is closed up like the church.
Doesn't go to every dogfight in town,
but likes Super-Chic fried wings.
He won't let poor kinfolks park
their jalopies in front of his spread.

At Pioneer Cabins - $15 - No TV - Buster Kidd
picks up trash with a nail on a broom handle.
His eyes, frantic from abuse, have no rest.
Social services says no, never mind.
These children adjust, come to terms.

The owner-operator of the Dixie Dream Motel sits
behind the picture window of the Pink Restaurant,
watches a scrawny teen-ager scratch "Trust Jesus"
on the wall beside the pay phone. It takes hours.

L. Kate Kelly Thomas

At Eye Level

We carved a heart, our names
and "I love you"
on a sweet gum.
My youthful eye pictured
the gum growing tall,
lifting our pledge skyward.

I thought that ivory-billed
woodpeckers would cling
to its trunk and drum
a serenade on its elevated heart.
I visioned mockingbirds
rehearsing their love lyric
from that magnificent "I love you."

Then, through the years,
I watched this engraved tree
bud from its top, while our heart,
our names, and "I love you"
remain at eye level.

Inzer Byers

Sodhouse Woman: 1868

Always a wind blowing here --
hot off scorching summer earth,
or freezing blue over deep-drifted snow.
Soddy can hold warmth enough
to keep back winter blasts,
but what gives cool from summer blaze?
Back east, I took my pride
in well-kept house. But here
inside the soddy, wind-borne dust
settles a thin gritty film over all.
Dust and silence.

Two years ago my only child,
so small in her make-shift coffin.
Ever since, this roof
weighs heavy upon me,
and an awful emptiness
reaches to the far horizon.
All is silence, silence --
except for the soughing wind
in drying prairie grass.

Everything here wears
a small white face.

Peggy B. Ferris

Phoenix

If I dream no dream to reality
Or 'grave an image in stone,
Pen No Note by the Muse's rote
Or lyrics for my song -
When returned to dust, then I Must, I Must,
With restless spirit rise
To fling a flaming arrow through the morning skies.

Leon Hinton

The Other Side

Five years old again, lost in darkness
parents and brothers call
from the other side of the stream.

"Richard, Richard!" He tries to
reach them. Hands lunge in the dark.
Each one says, "Take me.
I'll pull you across."

Just as he touches his father's fingers
he is sucked back into a hole
and falls down, down, down.

His seventy-five-years-old emaciated body
stretches out -- a long white ribbon
under the sheet.

Faces hover. "I thought he was gone."
"His heart did stop."

A prisoner in this clean, well-lit hell
constantly attacked by white-clad,
grim-faced devils with needles, pills,
tubes, enemas, robbing him of dignity,

they don't understand
when he talks to people on the
walls and ceiling,
refuses food and pills, has accidents
and mostly longs for the other side.

Betty R. Sigmon

With Apologies to True Blue Rednecks

What would my Country Club friends say
if they could see me now:
Squat on my heels to
discuss the crops and weather,
ride through fields
astride a Massey tractor
instead of my walking mare,
collect adjustable caps
from Roundup, Dekalb and Ford,
even got a wide belt with a Rebel buckle.

>   ...turning redneck...

Own a pickup truck with roll bars,
gun rack and chrome wheels,
packed the debutante dresses to
wear Wranglers everywhere I go,
have chiggers in places I
can't scratch in public.

>   ...definitely becoming a redneck...

Sold the luxury car to
drive a '68 Cuda
with a lopping cam and
150 MPH speedometer,
gave up tennis for drag racing,
order BBQ instead of steak,
Conway and Willie are taking
my tape player from Tchaikovsky.

>   Change back?
>   You gotta be kiddin

Next week

>   I'm having my name put

>   on the back of my belt

C. Pleasants York

Mademoiselle Frost

A crystalline Southern belle
crochets silver lace doilies,
then talcum powders the azaleas
and rustles her crinoline petticoats
as she curtsies to the morning.

Mary Wilmer

Singer

When I moved here without you,
I brought my sewing machine,
sewed up a batch of curtains
to make this house my own.
Remembered how, once before, I made
curtains for our first home,
sewed all night long,
waiting to hear your car turn
into the drive,
your cough as you walked
across the lawn from the garage.
Remembered stitching baby clothes,
little smocked dresses, debutante gowns,
making signal flags for our new boat
and sailors' shirts on those long weekends
when you went to the boat alone;
hoping that somehow the stitches
would hold you.
Remembered that last night
when I saw you cry for the first time
and we wept together,
closer than we'd been in years.
How you walked to the car
the next morning
not looking back.
Remembered buying this machine
one evening after too much wine,
wondering if it was worth the price.

W. Steven Williams

The Preacher's Wife

The people watched him lift his hands
in evangelical display...
> (She only saw the gentle hands
> that brushed her tears away).

They heard his voice as he spoke
in tone austere and deep...
> (She heard the voice that spoke her name
> while he lay fast asleep)

The people listened as he prayed
and lifted spirits high...
> (She prayed that it was only she
> who saw the grease-spot on his tie).

Janet Lee Warman

Widow

The woman on the screen speaks
of her dead husband watching
from heaven. She hopes he is.
The woman on my right touches
the rings on her left hand,
shudders slightly. Her grief,
passed like a communion plate,
settles with me. I hold it;
it is smooth, weighted,
the core of what she cannot say.
I want to carry it for her.
Never having lost, I walk easier,
have strength to haul dead things.
She sits tall in the air around her,
gathers the scattered fragments
of pain, sets both of us alone.

Billie Varner

It's Hard to Mend a Broken Heart

If our bones are broken—
they can be promptly mended
and grow strong as before
that ladder we ascended,
but this one thing—
—we must impart
it's hard to mend—
—a broken heart.
If a heart is diseased
or misses a beat—
we can call in the specialist
for him to treat—
but if a heart is broken
it's a fragile thing!
there's no Doctor to call
—to ease the pain.
So the broken heart
—has to mend instead
by proving, though fragile
—it's strong as lead.
We can then go on living
though it's never the same,
we will doubtless be stronger
for having won the game.

Gypsy Travis

To My Child, Dying

for Eprielle Yvette Hardin
February 10, 1965 - January 16, 1991

I carry around your dying
in my chest and some days
it expands so it nearly chokes
me. I cannot fix your crippled
wings and I cannot fly myself.
You call for your doctor as you
lose your supper, but your eyes
say to me that you know
he can help you no more than I.

The goodbye to come is not
the hardest part of all this.

I wonder how I'll be able to
pack up your quarter of a century
and store it in my own years, and
what will be my life without you?

Anne F. Stuck

To My Brother on His 65th Birthday

Like you
the October sun
gives gentle warmth
in its retreat.
It is both staunch and weak.
The feckless squirrel,
a few birds,
soak up its afterglow.
But briefly!
There is a wisdom
in the burrowing seeds
about departures.
And yet,
I can't let go.

I hear only
old reproaches
in the bare trees
the wind broaches,
their scrapes and creaks.
I hear just
songs dead crickets
sang before our autumn,
which you ignore.
And yet you come,
arms heaped with
cool mums -
curled gold -
to my door.

Luther Stirewalt

To Edna St. Vincent Millay

On the One Hundredth Anniversary of Her Birth, 1892-1992

I do not memorize Millay.
I cannot hear her sigh and sound
in fading echoes of her moods.
Fleshless tone will not again
clothe Eurydice in flesh.

I shall ever ask my heart:
 what was her intonation,
 what variant,
 did she whisper or exclaim,
 -- our last embrace?

I know Millay by heart
but not verbatim,
an "unremembered lad"
 --and no regret--
who yet will lay his arm
beneath her head till morning.

D. Elaine Stanberry

The Orb Weaver

Sun glittered on the artist's glossy
Black body, complimented with yellow
And an intricate grey web of silk lace
As morning dew added its clear sparkle.

The diligent artificer toiled long,
Intently absorbed in a delicate task
Which nature designated to her kind;
Like Arachne, she used her art well.

Larger and larger grew the fine art piece
Like a crocheted cloth styled by craftsmen
Till, proud as an aesthete, she viewed her work,
Which beauty-barren man destroyed fast.

Long legs crawled away from artistry ruined,
Pain hidden under fear for her body.

Amy Spanel

Loyal to His Royal

Brightly he smiles in his bow tie
Upon this gray, wintry day:
Gently speaking to those who seek
Him: Pilot of his paper,
Captain of Poetry, Mr. Sam T. Ragan
Stays loyal to his Royal --
Steering the helm of editorials,
Pecking away upon round,
Manual keys -- still feeling
The zeal for correspondence
"I get fired-up these days,"
Says he, a sage shake
From this modest corner
Of publisher's quarters --
Reassuring the seeker
While the smell of ink permeates:
That yes, this Mr. Ragan
Prevails. Yes, his love
Of Literature is unshakeable.
Yes, he presides even while
The other Reagan helmed 8 years --
Even with Senator Helms, still --
This Mr. Ragan runs a kind ship.
The rich do not get richer under him.
Loyal to his Royal, he
Pounds away upon round, shiny keys --
My heart beats faster when he smiles --
He who infuses renewal and sunlight
Into my life -- the Irradiant Mr. Ragan.

Sharon A. Sharp

Mother to Daughter

As you learn about men,
Explore boldly the differences
That set you apart, seeming to suggest
Two worlds and visions, tricking you
Into believing that variance in form
Divides souls, hearts and minds.

Explore: taste, touch, smell, see
The curves, lines, and folds, the skin-soft
Stubble-flecked angularity and aroma of
Maleness. Give of your pleasure,
Take of his pleasure; revel and be free.

As you learn about men,
Confront clearly the differences
That bring you together, seeming to refute
Any notion of conquest, lulling you
Into forgetting that flesh can be weapon
And your memories a prison.

Confront: disdain, deny, refuse, reject
Any who mockingly leer at your presence,
Who boast of power as they grab and press,
Breath searing, while they unzip and tear
At your clothes, sure of prevailing.

As you learn about men,
Demand that he who waits see in your body
The beauty of his own, pulsing with life, eager.
Listen for his soft sobs in the quiet of night
As he weeps for his own kind who defile passion
And negate the pure wholeness in differences.

Susan Rose

Effie and Ernes'

Effie ain't never said much
'bout being marriet to Ernes'
and him adyin'. But yestiddy mornin' early
I went over to her house to take her
some tomato seedlings she said she wantet.

We was standin' by the back steps
lookin' toward the old red barn at the peach tree,
ain't been pruned in years
but from the steps looked real pretty,
all them pink blooms 'longside that faded red barn
wit' the sun comin' up bright on 'em
and the cool mornin' air like a little shawl
awrappin' its arms 'round us.

Effie's eyes got kind of misty and she said real low,
"Ernes' thought you had to be asleepin'
or either adoin' somethin' in bed.
I triet to tell him but jus' plumb give up.
He couldn't never git it th'ough his head
that lots o' times I jus' wantet him
alayin' there 'longside me, awake
but not sayin' nothin' and not doin' nothin',
maybe touchin' feet a little.
Ernes' didn't never git it th'ough his head."

Eleanor Rives

Platinum Child

"The child is father of the man"
                    -- Wordsworth

Gentle as rain at dawn
she offers me her arm
in fear that I might fall,
cautions me to slow my pace
brings sweet surprises
to my simple spread.

This platinum child
who ran me such a race
scattered stones and laughter
in her path, her spirit free
as windchimes. Cried teen-tears
at her own rule-breaking, crept
to my bedside, whispered
"Are you mad at me?"

She asks now "Are you tired?
Can you walk a little farther?"
serves me herbal tea and gingersnaps
brings grandchildren to kiss
my wrinkled cheek and asks about
"the olden days."

When was the turning point?
Which was the drop of time
that overflowed the cup? Do
scales unbalance themselves?
When did this child become
my mother? I don't remember
                    ....can't remember.

Sandra Redding

Ascension

for Mary Hood

The commissioned artist
sits beside the highway
sketching a dead dog
its hind legs flattened to vermillon.

Pressing charcoal to paper
she sketches the dog a nose, then begins the eyes --
the easiest feature, she decides
for the closed lids
keep reality
from interfering with what she wills.

The old man who owned the pointer
crushes his cigarette.
"Her name was Gypsy," he says.
"Best hunting bitch
a man could wish for. Just yesterday
she treed a possum."

The artist
sensing that something of the man
belongs always with the pointer
tips her brush with pink, cerulean, then violet
surrounds the doghead
with its final aura.

John Moses Pipkin

Pomegranate

In still-life you emanate mystery,
Recalling equally a bulb, a root,
A sachet vase from ancient Araby --
Sheer <u>exotica</u> in a flesh-red suit.
To unlock you, I must desecrate you,
See you bleed magenta, suck the winy
Liquor from your fleshy seeds -- to know too
Why Hades gave you to Persephone.
For in that nether world of memory,
Where Lethe's waters bear off everything,
Must lodge some sight or touch or fantasy,
Forgotten but for your remembering.
Taste and recall, Eternity and time,
Cupped for a poet's pittance in my rhyme.

Charles Phillips

Gifts

Like a magician,
I would pluck
From air
A rose;

Like a genie,
Dazzle you
With gold;

Like a god,
Descend with fire
To serve.

But being only me,
I mold images
With words.

Pale at midday
Like the moon,
They may glow
For you at last
When dark enfolds
Your solitude.

Keith S. Petersen

Jail Visiting Hours

Above the metal panel, through the glass,
Your hair, your eyes, the tops of nose and beard,
These only, and the words the shield let pass
Between us, grudgingly, as if it feared
That you would slip out with them -- which it did
And worked to stop, and stopped. Time ticked away
While mouths, behind the metal safely hid,
Said all that grief and awkwardness could say.

Reality was bad enough. The dream
Was worse. We sat in comfortable chairs
And talked, and touched -- which made your prison seem
A den, a tavern even, free of cares --
Till, suddenly, they wrestled you away
And beat you senseless to the startled floor,
While helpless and too horrified to stay,
I tried to leave, and failed. There was no door.

Joseph F. Patterson, Jr.

Black and White Picture
in a Solid Gold Frame, 1944

Young and in love and parents to be
They sat on the sand
Side by side. Smiling, touching
In the warm sunlight

A special day at Laguna Beach.
Shielded from time by mystic allure!

The war seemed far away that day.
Her long ride home on the crowded troop train,
Her term almost in sight,
A nightmare yet to be dreamed.

The years apart,
The dangers waiting,
Were hidden by the curtain
While the set was being changed.

The lieutenant and his bride
Living that day alone.
The future forgot.

The sand was caked.
A dry river bottom.
The breakwater behind
Unkempt and uncaring.

But nothing would
change their happy smiles.
On the beach at Laguna
And in love!

Joseph Antonio Palladino

Paradise Garden

We walked in our gardens dark
Hearts beating each in its own rhythm
Each pathway different leading to
Journeys with life's teaching

We learned to laugh, to cry
To search we must
We came to our gardens unaware
We came expectant, we came afraid
Our journeys not complete

We grew to love each other
We trusted, believed he and she was I
For we are all one in the universe

And the journeys we take
The pathways we traverse
Lead us all together to our awareness

Our hearts now
Beat together as one
We enter awareness, we enter
Paradise Garden.

Lula Little Overton

Vision

Say not I had "a lover's quarrel with life,"
but that a love affair smote swift as blight:
that life like <u>incubus</u> deflowered me,
that passionate involvement spent my youth;
Say not I entered into mortal strife,
but that I labored in earth's fields with sight
upon the sun. Say that the grey-brown sea
washed off the scales that hid me from the truth;
Say that the sun-dimmed eyes sought out the moon
and watched it clear the cloud-filled skies at noon.
Or say my telescope was trained on stars
and that it saw beyond the mortal cage,
where infants toss their rattle-bombs in rage,
to look upon the unknown space where Mars
and Venus frolic. Take note that hope
magnetised my compass past man's scope.

Sallie Nixon

Apostrophe

I haven't written a poem for you,
    my son,
        in a very long time.

Once, in those fishnet years of disbelief
    and astonished anger,
        knowing you were not -

never could be - like others -
    knowing even a bright beach ball
        out of place with us -

and wanting to make some sense of it all,
    I wrote often and only for you,
        knitting a kind of normalcy into
            sonnets, rhymed couplets,
                precisely formed.

At 23, your death brought forth
    the longest poem - setting out,
        month by month, the year of your freeing -
        saying a celebration an ease
            to what cannot be eased.

But I must tell you, my son,
    I could not know how everlasting
        the clutch of disbelief
            or the need to make sense:

I imagine you now - perfectly whole -
    shining a happiness unknown to the living -
        able to speak -
            to say "Mother" -

I imagine it true.

Dee L. McCollum

Father's Love

Father weighed us once a month
And totaled up the pounds
Then he weighed the dog and cat
(As silly as that sounds)
He then included their weight, too,
And with pride and joy he'd say,
"Hmmm. Yes, I do believe
Here's what I have today:
There's thirty-five and forty-eight
And Jim weighs eighty-nine,
Spot and Puss weigh twenty-four
And all these pounds are mine!"
Father loved us not by age
Nor virtues that he found
He gathered all his children in
And loved us by the pound.

J. R. McCartney

Shadows of the Silent Screen

I had a piece of crystal once --
the projector lens from Wonderland.
Through it flowed images
that had condensed on the silent screen.
Focused in the stable loft,
it seared wood to make initials and dates.

> Galleons burning; the hortator beating;
> the splendor of the son of Hur
> entering the tent of Ilderim to claim
> the white stallions that would chariot him to glory.

Dust motes, swirling in the lens cone,
blackened to cinders.

> Trucks in parade formation; a boy,
> hot-eyed, throwing shoes and kisses,
> moving against the helmeted crowd,
> calling, "Melisande."

I heard in the stable loft -- "Melisande,"
breaking the silence.

I broke the lens and buried it.

Dug up, some years later, the pieces
softened by the soil were faintly violet.
I heard again -- "Melisande,"
but also a cough, and I saw a skull.

Morrison Myers

Grandma

Grandma
80 pounds
of German, English, and Dutch
rolled into a rock throwing
hawk killing
weasel shooting
commander of little boys
she took to work at an early age
swinging a mean hoe
harvesting everything in sight
nary a weed got to grow up

after she became
too old
to work with a hoe
too blind to pick
she shelled, shucked, sliced
did everything it took to can
but
I bet in heaven
they gave her a poke of snap seed
and a brand new hoe

Barbara J. Mayer

Souvenirs

You brought me a German music box,
deerskin bird house, parsley ring,
sent a postcard every day
from some storybook place
where you travelled light
without the baggage of a child.

When I grew older, I went with you
learned the pull of places far from home,
collected cedar boxes, tomahawks, a snapshot
of a dog leaping between two rocks,
and in my teens, letters from boys
I hid away from you.

When I found mountains, I wanted them
ranged like a mural on the wall.
I moved to the foothills, leaving you
miles behind. Now I find pink
dogwoods bearing Easter crosses,
a fiddle's wail on a moonless night.

None of this can be packaged.
Instead I send you porcelain dolls
made in Carolina, one in a striped
muffler, another in lace and pearls.
They perch on your mantel in pouty perfection,
mimicking grandbabies I can't give you.

Roy Manning

Mothers are Marvelous

Long ago I understood
Little things that mama did
Like eating chicken necks and feet
And serving good parts to us kids.

She mostly wore old faded clothes
Which she had no time to press
But she always saw to it
That we were clean and neatly dressed.

Sometimes when we chopped cotton
And the grass was tough and thick
She hoed her row and ours too
And let us play off sick.

Mama never talked much
And she was seldom heard
To tell us that she loved us
In just so many words.

But we knew how mama felt
She showed us every day
Sweet talk doesn't count for much
Compared to loving ways.

Nona Madison

Mother Teresa

She takes her cue from One who said that we
Could serve Him best by meeting mankind's needs.
Her ministrations, done so quietly,
Call no attention to her loving deeds.
While others vie for fame and power and wealth
And chant their creeds and pray their pious pleas
She feeds the poor and nurses back to health
Malnourished bodies ravaged by disease.

Needs are so great within just one small realm
We falter in despair, yet one lone nun
Won't let a hopeless spirit overwhelm.
With love, she helps just one - and one - and one.
She lives her faith and demonstrates her creed.
No time for fame - for she has lambs to feed.

Helen Cornwell Logan

Always Yours, Elizabeth

I found your picture, Elizabeth,
Still in its gold frame
Inside his desk drawer (the one he always locked).
Your eyes are so soft and luminous, eyes of one in love.
Your lips are parted just enough
To curve into that tender smile.
I like the soft swirling look of golden hair about
Your face.
There were letters there too,
Tied up with pieces of string
(the kind he always kept in his pocket with pipe
and tobacco).
Do I imagine a faint whisper of tobacco lingers?

I won't open your letters, Elizabeth,
They belong to him and you.
Love is like faith in God -- it's yours alone.
The desk is mine now.
He's gone (I'm sure you know)
But this drawer will still be his.
As I turn the key I still see your lovely
Lips smiling, your eyes so filled with love.
You wrote on the picture,
"Always yours, Elizabeth."
Now you will be.

Jane K. Lambert

The Unknown

Welcome to this world, newborn babe
    vulnerable, invincible
    hope of tomorrow
we give to you
the burdens of our earth's survival -
        How many angels can dance
        on the head of a pin?

Mary Ann Kattah

Metamorphic Revelations

Tonight - beads of introspective sweat burn
Burn droplets into inevitable ashes.
I am thinking, if I could capture the laughter of my soul
And pour it over my scorching pain,
I could **BE** once again.
I sink deeper. Warning: if I think too much
I may metamorphose into knowing more.

I, unafraid, wait. Tree frogs chant a hypnotic OMmmmmmmm
Into lost crevices of me, beyond where no other eyes can see.
Touching my tongue over my lips, and wanting to taste more
I wait.

The "more" is about my faithful kindness (still intact!)
That will not break - this morning, or any other.

Happily I pull my blushing beliefs over my shoulders.
Against **ALL** who say - that given certain circumstances
One must surrender oneself.

Listen! Urgent cries are protesting from
Edna St. Vincent Millay's tomb.
She understood the living/dying conflict.
I musn't hand over my breath of bloom
To another's belief that deadens my own.

Misty shafts rise over a joyous willow, no longer weeping.
I hop on this ethereal escalator into a new day.
The same distinct constant, yet fresh and different,
As my strength resurrected with each approach.

Leave fear under this night's moving moon. Leave it there...
Wrenching and whimpering in the grave of powerlessness.
Knowingly nurture emancipating **CHOICES**!
Become them more fully, share them with <u>sane</u> sameness.

Ellen Turlington Johnston-Hale

A Blessing

He was spared the tubes that would have
strung his days into a
chain. A blessing.

how he slipped away.
Merciful, so quietly it was, like
feathers.

Now the safety net woven at his
death by sanctions
spun by sympathizers to make her

loss seem bearable
wears away, shredded by
images sharp as kitchen knives:

Sunday pancakes, after
supper walks...
How could he

leave her to wake and
walk alone, to try to fall
asleep?

She struggles to remember
a blessing,
merciful,

to stop her catapult to anger that
pierces dusk, shatters every dawn,
hollows days and nights to hopeless husks.

Tom Johnson

The Deals We Struck

When we had, at last, had our fill with each other,
we moved, still vibrating, to the corners --
the neutral corners of the bed.
We sat apart, without speaking,
as if to reclaim
something not shared.

The last afternoon light through the window,
the sky being repainted in darker grays
by long brush strokes, east to west,
we became aware of our separateness,
our nakedness, and reached
to pull the sheets around us.

You took your hand and smoothed away
the wrinkles between us,
as God may have done to the Great Plains,
but lifting his hand too quickly
left the Rocky Mountains.

Under the yellow slice of moon much past
its fullness, your whisper stayed
just beyond my fingertips.
I watched the cool shiver
of your shoulder.
I should have known then:

some promises
are contracts that expire
the moment they are made.

Ruth Ilg

Cancer Ward

A Pied Piper on Rounds,
he pontificates
in his untouchable white smugness
of doctoring
to his mesmerized patients
and students alike.

Diseased bodies quell their agonies,
praying to find a speck of hope
against all hope
within
the manicured charade each day.
Impatiently,
they wait in awe and expectation...
as children would
to see the freakshow at the fair;
but here they are the freaks
with tumors nesting in their flesh
and parasites feeding from within.

The Piper's pipe grows silent as he leaves.
The magic is gone.
Until tomorrow.

Nancy Humphries

Balance

You live in the air,
and I in the sea.
I disperse with the tides
and you on the breeze.

One is a backdrop,
the other, a stage.
Canopy to foundation
No connection is made.

Air in the water
Moisture in the sky
Tears on your cheek
or dust in my eye.

A tangible grasp is impossible with you
To drown you in a teaspoon, is my best ruse.
Asleep or awake, you're an ethereal dream.
I tumble down stones into flowing streams.

Needed by nature, for life to begin.
Coming together on the head of a pin.
One to start, the other to sustain,
Balancing together, the wind and the rain.

Knowing of each other is almost enough
But coming together is usually too rough.
Tempest in a teacup or hurricane on the sea
We need to be seperate to exist peacefully.

A gentle rain, a lilting breeze
Our very best features for others to see.
Combining the forces, malevolence assured
But together, a balance, the world will endure.

William M. Hendricks

Noble Words

*"After all is said and done, love
is more than noble words."*

She sits there beside her mother listening,
watching the dusk fade from the window sill.
They remember past harvests when her mother
strode fiercely about the dusky farm
Strapped behind an old hunched mule
with cropped ears and a hide as hard
as dry brown varnish drawing straight
rows in the red dirt while the youngest
of seven sucked the nape of her neck.
Hurrying home to help her eldest daughter
fire up the stove and fix the dinner table
too tired to rest for a while,
she just worked on a bit longer.

Now her thick-boned body can rest
among soft sheets and pillowcases
in padded comfort. The earthen face coughs
and shakes, and her daughter rises to prop
pillows around her. Carefully, slowly
she turns her mother, inspecting the ulcers
chiselled on her buttocks.
Deliberately, she folds a white gauze pad,
pressing its softness into the depths
of flesh as they gossip about children
and children's children, kinfolk
and a homeplace far away.

Carol Bessent Hayman

Reflections From the Castle

As we grow old we come to realize
great strength and energy are part of youth.
In battered turrets, filled with countless lies,
We wait alone remembering the truth
that beckoned like a path, shining and clear,
Across a world that, yesterday, we owned.
Where now the dream belief made more-than-dear?
Where all the hopes and plans? The games we've won
are faded flags around the tower walls;
Our arms grow tired, our weapons mould and rust.
The sun descends, the chill of evening falls;
We search for love, for deeds and hearts to trust.

What have we learned and left? What lamp or book
will light and justify the way we took?

Maureen Ryan Griffin
To Any POW

"Their eyes were dull, like a wild animal's
that had just been tamed.... These men were tortured."

It's January, and if you could remember --
between the copper wire that cuts into your flesh
and the statements they force from you --
you'd know what that means. Cold,
and the sun slanting low.

I've taken to walking, staring at trees
against the winter sky. I don't know how to feel
about this war. I do know how I feel about
you. I want to bake you cookies, lay my body
on yours -- would anything

make you forget? But I can do nothing
except to notice the quince
in bloom, its sprawling branches
a Japanese still life,
clusters of five rosy petals

a testament to asymetry as they loosen
from those pregnant buds, as the petals
cup the stamens so lovingly,
bend backward to expose
each throat. And in the woods

a leggy rhododendron grows
heartily in a mulch of dead leaves.
I don't know how to feel about
that either. I only know my young son
has just discovered evergreens,

and as I show him textures, hues --
from lacey to coarse, bristly to finespun,
lush to tender to deep --
I do so in your name.

Kathy Brannon Green

I Am Woman

I am woman.
I look in the mirror
and am discouraged by what I see there.
Fine lines are beginning to form.
The bloom of youth is no longer there.
Still, I am woman.

I am woman.
The body in which I live
has changed throughout the years.
My physical vitality is no longer the same.
Yet my feelings and hopes and dreams
are still within me, and
I am woman.

I am woman.
I remind myself
that those who care for me
see the qualities
under the appearance, which is skin deep.
I am no less
because of the passing of the years.
I am woman.

I am woman.
Please, see the person that I am.
See me.
Look beyond what
you can see with your physical eyes.
Take the time to know me.
I am still of worth.
I am me, and
I am woman.

Jacquie Gray

The Lady in the White Rattan Chair

She sits in a white rattan chair
on the screened porch
facing the sea.
'Tis twilight
as she sips her lemonade,
sits it on the
white tile coaster
embossed in gold.
It twinkles as the
light hits it,
as does the
gold-in-relief pin
on her lapel—
both gifts of love.
She sits in a white rattan chair
sips her lemonade and
watches the sunlight
play on the rippling waves.
The tide crashes in,
clutches an armful of
sand and runs away.
It seems to say,
Come play with me.
Colors play with the clouds—
like dainty pastel ribbons,
they weave a Maypole
as the sun quietly bows and
slips away.

Jean Cromer Gouveia

You Will Always Be There

Thoughts of you teased my mind today, attempting
to awaken long-forgotten memories
of joyous moments we once shared, long past now

We were so young, so eager, so unaware
of what this sometimes cruel world had in store
for two naive, unsuspecting optimists.

The wind blew a gentle breeze that sunny day
we sat in the shade of a sycamore tree
and promised to love each other forever.

Life was so good, the future so bright to us.
How could anything negate those positive
happy visions of the married life we'd share?

The cruelty of life that always affects
others then crushed our dreams without warning—
you died...our precious dreams died with you.

Memories of you linger, not forgotten
but simply buried deep within my brain, a
protection against too much pain and sorrow.

Though I love another, you are always near
for I feel your presence in the gentle breeze,
in the sunshine as I walk in the meadow.

Your soothing voice seems to beckon me towards
the shade of that beautiful sycamore tree
where I most strongly remember you, my love.

Elaine L. Goolsby

Widow

I know he's gone but
sometimes I still call to him.
Habits die hard, you know.
We were married sixty years.
Sixty years this June past,
after the crops were laid by.
No, I'm not scared by myself,
Buddy's with me. He was Sam's dog.
I'm not scared. See that picture
over the mantel? Ain't it pretty?
We got that right after we married.
I used to dream I could run right
into that sunset! And this rocking chair.
Look at them wooden pegs. I got
two of these when I was a girl.
We called them courting chairs.
Sam fell down on the floor right here.
Buddy curled up close beside him.
I called the Rescue Squad but
I knew it was no use. I knelt down
and put his hand on Buddy's head.
Buddy's grieving. Dogs grieve too,
you know. Dogs grieve too.

Helen Goodman

Rag Doll

Eager hands awaited his
orders. Feet danced at
his command. Her lips
were fixed in a heedless
smile and innocent eyes
stared into Neverland
where she saw only the
handsome toy soldier.
Her naked heart cried,
"I love you," but never
heard its echo.

Then one day he left.
Wearied of playing house,
he split and went in search of
prettier toys. Fortunately,
her gray gingham apron
covered the wound where
he nearly tore her guts out.

However, that slamming door
must have exuded magical
vibrations, for this docile
doll suddenly realized she
was growing a spine.

She found his <u>Complete</u>
<u>Do-It-Yourself Manual</u>
and proceeded to change
the locks.

Vivian H. Gainer

Everyone Tries for the Big Guy

One conquest after another
I won-I made the rules
No Strings Attached
And so I'm caught, I fell
in love
I strain all bonds
Near sell my soul
To have what can't be had...
Except for stolen moments
I pay the price with interest.
I asked "What is the interest rate?"
I don't know
I guess I'll learn at a later date.

Colleen H. Furr

Philemon

"Grant this one request, that...

neither of us be left without the other."

-- from the myth "Baucis and Philemon"

Twice now he has awakened me
with an abrupt shake, called my name,
asked, "Are you all right?"
Each time I have answered
and gone back to sleep smiling.

I understand this sudden fear,
know how long the seconds stretch,
how loud the silence grows
when you watch for movement,
listen for the sound of breathing.

My fear comes in the mornings
but more patient than he,
I stand by the bed,
put out a hand to feel for warmth,
the rise and fall of breath,
then go to the kitchen to make coffee
and begin the new day.

Rebecca J. Finch

Communion

She lies at the end of the aisle,
her brown face fixed in pink satin.
>   From somewhere, she whispers to me.
>   "You just as well to laugh as cry."
>   Last July she stood beneath a writhing web
>   matted on a cherry branch. With hands on hips
>   to square her roundness, she said to Pop
>   "I'll cook, wash, mop
>   But I don't do caterpillars."
One gold tooth emblazoned each smile, each word.
>   "When my people overcame
>   I was sleeping on the couch...
>   You just as well to laugh as cry."
Now, paper fans depicting Martin Luther King sweep
gnats from air too thick to breeze through window screens.
Whirling blades above clip the preacher's drone.
>   "You must love one another."
The Sisters and Brothers surely wonder
who I am.
That lone white woman who quietly cries amidst
their hallelujahs.
The electric organ roars.
A clear-eyed baby wails.
The choir claps and sways.
Notes ricochet off concrete walls
>   "What a friend we have in Jesus." Amen.

Charles Edward Eaton

Sun Helmet

The construction worker with the glistening hair
Is supple as a plant in all his thoughts,
Watering himself secretly with sweat.
His helmet, colored like a daffodil,
Takes and turns away the sun's hard kiss.
There's iron in this garden and deep, damp roots;
In the metallic light, a dipperful
Of water satisfies like jungle rain.

The structure rises but it cannot delve;
It is light rising from the worker's hand.
One block from another mocks the glare,
The sun fights back as it has done
Since Babylon. Only a plantlike man
Can insinuate his secret power—
A passing cloud, and one remembers caves,
How the brain simmered paintings on the wall.

Under the yellow helmet, the head cools
A little, but the torso's rivers run—
What is the mix of solid, soluble?
Enormous blistering days and deep, dark nights
Contend along the narrowest catwalk,
The helmet arbitrates how high we go—
Without sun, no one would ever take heart,
A little darkness keeps the soul alive.

Grace DiSanto

Elegy for an Unborn Grandchild

You are dead; you would have
been my grandchild. I want

to weep but there is no body. I
want to face pictures to the wall,

nail a wreath to the door, but there
is no body. No ashes. Your

soul is hovering off life
in the wings waiting to light another.

And as another you will walk
to school, pass our empty house, break

the stillness of the yard. And in
winter sunsets, when days drop flames

like fireworks, we shall watch you
pass, coming without ever coming near.

Ann Deagon

La Giudecca

If it be not now, yet it will come.

We all end up in Hell. The smiling boy
invites us onto the motor launch.
Three hundred lire is all it takes.
We cross the water. Tourists all.
Under the boat the garbagewoman sea
scours sunken landings. At the Giudecca
we disembark. We wait before
the barred door. Above, a mirror
eyes us like thieves. The maid pulls
the cord. Inside, a black hound
cavorts. We skirt the pallid plants
and mount toward day. Here is the palace
I promised. At morning light will rise
like mist from the lagoon. At night the black
dog gulps down the sun.
There is no other place to live.

In the estuary he lies becalmed.
His bed is motorized, jolts and subsides
with every tide. The mast is steel.
Sweet water enters him and salt comes out.
He is bound to the mast. He hears me singing.
Dante, you had it wrong. Hell's not for traitors.
In la Giudecca Satan chews
us. And marriage means
precisely that we see each other dead,
always climbing, always looking back:
the secret clause in all our undertakings.

Vera Dancy

The Rose

Written after reading a biography of Rose Kennedy

when only a tiny bud, all sensed the rarity
discovered in this forgotten corner of the
garden- the exquisite petals, so delicately
edged, were lined with steel; and so the
Gardener took up this Rose, placed her deep
into good, sweet earth among His other special
ones; nurtured her, cherished her, not just for
her unique beauty without, but more for her
self-less heart within from which she shared
His generous gifts with all who touched her
life; in time she became a glorious bloom and
soon tiny buds around her appeared in whom she
found great joy and daily thanked the Gardener
for His tender care, His many kindnesses to her-
      then horrible storms that rained blackness
      beat down upon the garden; the Rose watched
      as first one then another of her youthful
      buds was wrenched away; she called to the
      Gardener and He came after each storm passed,
      taught her how to pull from the core of
      courage which held her upright while weaker
      ones wilted away; her petals should have
      fallen long ago, but she stands with all
      intact; her quiet dignity is renowned; all
      marvel when passing her place in His Garden.

Robert J. Collins

People Of One Fire

We are still among you
We are one fire,
Warrior ghosts among your buildings
Ghosts in teepees in your parking lots
Spirit children playing
Under your river bridge.

Each year in those ancient times
When the Master of Breath
Still gave us life
At that time when a new-born moon
Silvered the ripeness of our sacred corn
We let our campfires die
And on that day sent proud sons
Like swift deer through the forest
To bring new flame
From the teepee of our chief,
For that we were called
People Of One Fire.

Still among you, we cannot leave
One with earth, one with sky
We are tied to you through all time
By a beaded string of centuries,
Bound to you by one fire.

Ed Cohen

The Big Horses

What did my granddad know
    That I don't know?
He had a woman for 42 years-
Mine leave after a few beers.
One day I had bought a tractor
And asked him to tell me
    what he knew.
He answered, "Percherons, Clydesdales,
    Suffolks and Shires"
Good horses, with hearts instead
    of tires,
And a woman who more than
    Loves,----Admires
That's what he told, and
    I guess, I forgot
For all that he had, I have not.
Now I'll remember--
    Percherons, Clydesdales
    Suffolks and Shires,
Great horses, with hearts instead
    of tires
And a woman who more than loves----Admires.

Shirley G. Cochrane

Getting There Ourselves

Our fathers have been gone so long we've almost
forgotten how they looked in double-breasted
pin-striped suits, how their eyes shone
behind rainbow-rimmed glasses. Sometimes
we can recapture their morning struts,
their homecomings to bourbon and branch water.

We see our mothers in their morning-glory aprons
bending to take lemon spongettes from 1930's ovens;
in our minds, that is -- actually only one is left
and she doing poorly in the nursing home built
where the Weaver's cows used to graze, relinquishing
their mortgaged milk for our tables.

We think of ourselves as the young crowd
even as we board the train for classmates'
funerals (a third one buried last week).
What's happened is that still in our youthful
regalia we've been tapped for the older
generation -- an honor we never really wanted.

Mollie Christie

Hubris

"To be as gods" -- the ageless, ceaseless cry,
To know, to see with new-enlightened eyes,
For this, the questing mind would dare defy.
-- And God clangs closed the gates of Paradise.
To break the bonds that bind flesh-feet to earth,
To feel the freedom ether-breathing brings,
Man soars in space, upborne by godlike worth.
-- And Phoebus hotly frowns on waxen wings.
To probe beyond this clay and seize the fire
That separates divine from mortal stock,
To this, the seeking soul would dare aspire.
-- And Zeus chains man's ambition to the rock.
Man's heedless heart yearns on, to dreams held fast;
He cannot, must not know the gods speak last.

Eileen Connell Cella

A Daughter's Gift

And so I assembled those little squares
Of woolen threads and yarn, which were a gift,
An afghan for my brother, her uncle.

I could have tossed them in a drawer to
Gather dust and moths, but I could not let
That last gift die so unworthy a death.

For this daughter had braved such odds and been
So valiant through years of balding despair,
The gift was a banner, a pennant of love.

Through summer months, she patiently knitted
Square after square and square after square of
Color, color which no longer filled her face.

And then the clicking, knitting needles stopped.

The squares lay restless to be united.
With heavy hand I finished this last gift
And sent it to my brother, her uncle.

Years later, a childless aunt cried out: Why,
Did you not keep it for yourself to hold,
To remember her hands upon the wool?

(The woolen shreds which now might be a shroud.)

Her wish, her hope, I could not extinguish
By locking those squares in some tiny cupboard,
Pulling them out and weeping over each,
Her spirit within those stitches entwined.
Completing the gift had become her life.
Mine -- was to hold her in my arms, forever.

Bette Burgess

From The City of Angels

On that sweltering July morning
A package arrived, neatly addressed to our son
Stuffed with mementos of your past
Pins, patches and ear plugs from your
National Guard days
Silver buttons from an old coat worn by
Great Grandpa Burgess in some long ago battle,
A tiny, faded, pink silk purse carried by
Grandma Whalen to parties in Spokane,
Thick woolen mittens knitted by a Branchfield aunt
For your dad when he worked on the railroad.
A nearly hairless paint brush used by
Charlie Russell as he painted his way
Across the old west.

There was even a plastic Pluto puzzle and a
Mickey Mouse bank with two old dimes
But most surprising was a small worn leather
Pouch that held your Notre Dame High ring
And your thick gold wedding band.

I watched your son's face as he touched
Each treasure, asking four year old questions,
Innocent in his need.
He fingered each piece over and over
Looking for that connecting thread
That broke so long ago.

George E. Beville

Lofty Dreams
A Seminarian's Nightmare

I dreamed I climbed a golden stair,
With scepter and with harp in hand,
And old Saint Peter waited there
To welcome me to Glory Land.
He led me to a massive hall,
And gathered there from every age,
So neatly stacked from wall to wall
Were books with finely printed page.

I stared in wonderment and awe
And prayed to find when I awoke
That I'd imagined all I saw;
That this was just a heavenly joke.
But then I heard old Peter say,
"You'd best start reading fast, my son.
The object of your quiz today
Demands you read them every one.

Your first assignment is a breeze:
Just briefly tell us on what wise,
At least a thousand pages please,
Did Bultmann demythologize.
Provide the title of each book
As penned by man since time began.
Discuss, in brief, the stance they took,
And name the authors every man."

Then questioning my whereabouts
I checked with Peter once again
To satisfy my surging doubts
Of just what place I'd landed in.
My name was called, to my surprise,
As from a lofty mountain pass,
And I awoke to realize
That I had slept through half the class.

Billye Canady Best

Laying On Of Hands
for Nellie at 88

His Mother, and Mine-in-Love,
reached with fragile fingers
to smooth my tense drawn temple,
stroke neck and shoulders
with tender, soothing touch;
spread scented talc in small swirls,
palms searching sections uncapitulated,
until my head fell gently back
to rest against her,
reduced to pliant putty.

Standing so in twilight,
she spoke of her bridesmaid's dress,
of daisies adorning her hair
for her sister's wedding, seventy summers ago;
then, gliding back with presents,
tossed a compliment -
that I have lovely shoulders for sunback dresses -
(I never knew!)
Supine, I spliced her memories onto mine,
restored by her laying on of hands.

Murray Benett

People and Poems

Some make me laugh,
Some make me cry.
Some shout at me,
And some whisper.
I don't know why.

Others hiss and mutter.
Them,
I don't understand
But
I do hear.

Others,
Most others,
Just gurgle
And I hear nothing.

People and poems.
Why?

Judith L. Benedetto

Eating Kiwi

I split
the stubbled oval
with one slice
hollow out
the pale
green flesh
white heart
black seed specks
offer you a few
dripping spoonsful
and the empty skin.